philharmonisches orchester berlin

the historic years 1913-1954

discography compiled by john hunt

philharmonisches orchester berlin
the historic years
1913-1954

John Hunt

© John Hunt 2018

ISBN 978-1-901395-35-8

Travis & Emery Music Bookshop
17 Cecil Court
London
WC2N 4EZ
United Kingdom.
Tel. (+44) (0) 20 7240 2129.
newpublications@travis-and-emery.com

Contents
introduction/*page 5*
guide to grammophon numbering system/*page 9*
recording venues/*page 10*
the discography 1913-1954/*page 11*
index of conductors/*page 313*
index of composers and their works/*page 327*
index of works by unidentified composers/*page 391*

PHILHARMONISCHES ORCHESTER BERLIN:
THE HISTORIC YEARS 1913-1954
AN INTRODUCTION TO THE DISCOGRAPHY

It was inevitable that, in my series of discographies devoted to Europe's leading orchestras, Berlin's Philharmonic (nowadays known as *Berliner Philharmoniker)* would demand inclusion. Having surveyed our own Philharmonia Orchestra (1987), Wiener Philharmoniker (2000), Sächsische Staatskapelle Dresden (2002) and Staatskapelle Berlin (2013), I now respond to the wishes of the many collectors of historical gramophone recordings with this one devoted to the early years of Berlin's Philharmonic. More volumes will of course be necessary in order to bring us right up to date, but this listing focuses on the important pioneer years starting with those very first records in 1913 and continuing up until the death in 1954 of the orchestra's most illustrious permanent conductor Wilhelm Furtwängler (the next volume will obviously cover the era of his successor Herbert von Karajan). Furtwängler himself was by choice not a prolific advocate of making records - many of his best ones stem from radio broadcasts - but he is surrounded in this discography by scores of other *maestri* (or *Kapellmeister*, as most of them would probably preferred to be called).

In Berlin as in London, the second and third decades of the twentieth century saw a thriving competition between record companies and the leading symphony

Introduction/continued

orchestras to commit the classical repertoire, as it was then known to concert audiences, to disc. Significant impulses came from the introduction of electrical (microphone) recordings around 1926-1927 (the previous acoustic method had greatly restricted the scope of what could be achieved). Then came the advent of tape recording, widely exploited during the years of the Nazi dictatorship, and leading in turn to the introduction of the long-playing record. Our discography thus embraces acoustic 78rpm, electrical 78rpm, 45rpm and 33.1/3 rpm records, the latter accomodating, for the first time, an entire symphony or concerto on one disc.

The competition which I mentioned was centred in the German capital around the *Philharmonisches Orchester* and the *Staatskapelle*. It has to be admitted that at the start of these pioneering years the *Staatskapelle* was the more enterprising in accepting repertoire offered by the record companies. For the Philharmoniker, Nikisch conducted only a few sessions before his untimely death in 1922, whilst Furtwängler, as already stated, was reluctant to commit to the mechanical recording process. Things were gradually beginning to change by the early thirties when the likes of Erich Kleiber, Bruno Walter, Jascha Horenstein and, later, Hans Schmidt-Isserstedt and Eugen Jochum started taking a serious interest in

Introduction/continued

studio work. The earliest years had seen a preponderance of short pieces, primarily operatic arias, but even in the 1930s the lighter side was not neglected: a common feature of the recording programme being the "potpourri" or "fantasy" of themes by composers both major and minor, as well as orchestral arrangements of music originally composed for a solo instrument.

I have also included in the discography various attempts to capture the orchestra performing on film, whether in newsreel footage or as background integrated into feature films. However, it is realised that some have not been traced, and also missing are those sound recordings known to have been made by the orchestra using pseudonyms.

The discography is divided into numbered sessions (001-497), many of which included a number of separate musical works. Each session is headed by recording date(s) and recording venues (wherever known), plus the name of the conductor in charge of that session (names of concerto or vocal soloists are entered after the details of each work). A left-hand column gives the basic matrix numbers, two for each 78rpm disc, whose main catalogue number follows in a second column: if only a single matrix number is shown, it can be assumed that the other side (coupling) contained a recording by an ensemble other than the *Philharmoniker*. Finally there follow the main known LP and CD re-issues for each work.

Introduction/concluded

A framework for this particular discography was already in place in the form of the invaluable exercise carried out in 1998-1999 by Michael H. Gray and published in the Japanese periodical *Classic Press*. Other colleagues who have contributed data or suggestions are John Baker, Roderick Krüsemann, Alan Newcombe and David Patmore.

<u>John Hunt 2018</u>

GUIDE TO GRAMMOPHON 5-DIGIT NUMBERING SYSTEM DURING THE SHELLAC ERA (78RPM DISCS)
as it applies to the discography of philharmonisches orchester berlin

30cm (12-inch) discs

15 000	19 000	21 000
27 000	35 000	36 000 (LV)*
45 000	57 000	65 000
66 000	67 000	68 000 (LM)*
69 000	72 000 (LVM/LVH)*	
90 000	91 000	
92 000	95 000	

categories 2400, 2900 and 7400 (all with prefix AVM) were added for the early music series (archiv produktion) introduced after the second world war

25cm (10-inch) discs

10 000	23 000	24 000
25 000	47 000	62 000 (L)*

*prefixes were added to signify the variable grade (longer playing) discs introduced after the second world war

PHILHARMONISCHES ORCHESTER BERLIN: THE RECORDING VENUES

admiralspalast	aeg factory
alte-jakob-strasse studio	alte philharmonie
bachsaal	beethovensaal
berliner dom	gemeindehaus dahlem
gemeindehaus zehlendorf	haus des rundfunks
hochschule für musik	jesus-christus-kirche
lichterfelder festsäle	lützowstrasse studio
maxim-gorki-theater	musikhochschule
odeon factory	olympia stadion
schillertheater	schumansaal
singakademie	staatsoper unter den linden
titania palast	wilhelmsaue studio
zwölf-apostel-kirche	

also various acoustic recording rooms in and around berlin

venues outside berlin

alexandria	baden-baden
bremen grosser glockensaal	cairo
granada	hamburg musikhalle
london empress hall	london queens hall
lugano teatro apollo	munich deutsches museum
paris theatre de l'opera	rome foro italico
turin sala del conservatorio	wiesbaden staatstheater

001/12-16 september 1913/grammophon acoustic sessions in berlin
alfred hertz
wagner parsifal prelude
1163   040772/040792/65896/69500
1160
1162   040773/040793/65897/69501
further 78rpm issues: hmv D 171-172/AB 63-64/ES 132-133
lp: emi RLS 768/1C137 53095-53099
cd: emi CDF 300 012/naxos 8.110049-110050/
berliner philharmoniker BPH 0601

wagner parsifal: act one verwandlungsmusik
1168   040778/040798/65899/69503
1161
further 78rpm issues: hmv D 172/AB 68
cd: naxos 8.110049-110050/berliner philharmoniker BPH 0601

wagner parsifal: karfeitagszauber
1169   040776/040796/65898/69502
1171
further 78rpm issues: hmv D 174/AB 65/ES 134
cd: naxos 8.110049-110050/berliner philharmoniler BPH 0601

wagner parsifal: act three verwandlungsmusik
1172   040775/040795/65897/69501
further 78rpm issues: hmv D 173/AB 64/ES 133
cd: naxos 8.110049-110050/berliner philarmoniker BPH 0601
original 6-digit issues were published in both single-sided and double-sided versions

002/10 november 1913/grammophon acoustic sessions in berlin
arthur nikisch
beethoven symphony no 5 in c minor op 67

1249	040784/040204/080509/69504/66274
1250	040785/040205/080510
1251	040786/040206/080511/69505/66275
1252	040787/040207/080512
1253	040788/040208/080513/69506/66276
1254	040789/040209/080514
1255	040790/040210/080515/69507/66277
1256	040791/040211/080516

further 78rpm issues: hmv D 89-92/AB 67-70
lp: perennial 2002/deutsche grammophon 2721 070/2740 259/ emi RLS 768/1C137 53095=53099/1C053 01466M
cd: symposium 1087/deutsche grammophon 453 8042/dutton CDBP 9784/pristine audio PASC 310

003/1913-1914/odeon acoustic sessions in berlin
camillo hildebrand
rubinstein toreador et andalouse; grieg peer gynt: solveig's song

XXB 5794	0-76428
XXB 5795	0-76429

wagner parsifal prelude and karfreitagszauber

XXB 5981	0-76434/0-6042/RX 104
XXB 5982	
XXB 5983	0-76435/0=6043/RX 105
XXB 5984	

mendelssohn ruy blas overture

XXB 5998	0-76442/0-6413
XXB 5999	0-76443

003/1913-1914/odeon acoustic sessions i/concluded
boccherini menuetto; weber-berlioz aufforderung zum tanz
XXB 6000   0-76440
XXB 6001   0-76441

wagner die meistersinger von nürnberg: orchestral arrangement of preislied; lohengrin act three prelude
XXB 6002   0-6041
XXB 6111

wagner tannhäuser overture
XXB 6005   0-6416/RX 111
XXB 6006
XXB 6007   0-6417/RX 112
XXB 6008

wagner lohengrin: procession to the minster
XXB 6023   0-53024/0-6127
XXB 6024   0-53025

beethoven egmont overture
XXB 6025   0-76426
XXB 6026   0-76427

wagner kaisermarsch
         0-76455/0-6196
         0-76456

saint-saens danse macabre
         0-76444/0-6197/RX 108
         0-76445

78rpm records with 5-digit numbers were single-sided discs

004/1921/grammophon acoustic sessions in berlin
max von schillings
schillings moloch: das erntelied
455	69556/65913
456	

schillings ingwelde act three prelude
457	69564/65919
458	

wagner der fliegende holländer overture; schillings mona lisa: ständchen des arrigo
469	69557/65914
470	
471	69558/65915
459	

wagner tannhäuser overture; tristan und isolde prelude
475	69559/65916
473	
476	69560/65917
502	
503	69561/65918
504	

005/1921/grammophon acoustic sessions in berlin
leo blech
wagner rienzi overture
482	69569/65879
483	
484	69570/65880

005/1921/grammophon acoustic sessions/concluded
grieg peer gynt suite no 1
485	69562/65876/vocalion 38009
486	
487	69563/65877/vocalion 38010
488	

bizet l'arlesienne: pastorale, intermezzo and menuet
520	69585/65814/65878
521	

006/1921/grammophon acoustic sessions in berlin
arthur nikisch
liszt hungarian rhapsody no 1 in f minor
639	69566/65906/vocalion 38006
640	
641	69567/65907/vocalion 38007
642	

lp: perennial 2002/deutsche grammophon 2721 070/emi 053 01466
cd: symposium 1087/zyx music 50242/dutton CDBP 9784/
berliner philharmoniker BPH 0601

berlioz le carnaval romain overture
643	69588/65908
644	

lp: perennial 2002/deutsche grammophon LPEM 19 078/2721 070
cd: symposium 1087/zyx music 50242/deutsche grammophon
459 0002/dutton CDBP 9784/berliner philharmoniker BPH 0601

16

007/1921-1922/grammophon acoustic sessions in berlin

leo blech

schubert symphony no 8 in b minor d759 "unfinished"

712	69597/66278
713	
714	69598/66279
715	
716	69599/66280

grieg in autumn overture

709	69599/66280
710	
711	69600/66281

reznicek donna diana overture

718	69570/65880
719	

wagner siegfried idyll

720	69571/65881/vocalion 38004
721	
722	69572/65882/vocalion 38005
723	

boieldieu la dame blanche overture

724	69573/65883
725	

auber fra diavolo overture

726	69574/65884
727	

008/1922/grammophon acoustic sessions in berlin
max von schillings
schubert rosamunde: ballet music no 1 and ballet music no 2
799   69575/65920
800

weber euryanthe overture
801   69576/65921
802

009/1922/grammophon acoustic sessions in berlin
hermann abendroth
strauss tod und verklärung
963   65871/69584
964
965   65872/69585
966
967   65873/69586
968

johann strauss die fledermaus overture
61   65870/69577
107

beethoven symphony no 1: first movement
63   65874/69591
64

18
010/1922/grammophon acoustic sessions in berlin
emil cooper
liadov nänie; glazunov scherzo (totentanz)
47 69606/65905
50

glazunov prelude from the middle ages suite
48 69605/65904
49

rimsky-korsakov le coq d'or: introduction and cortege
51 69601/65900
52

liadov kikimora
53 69602/65901
54

mussorgsky night on bare mountain
55 69603/65902
56
57 69604/65902

011/august-october 1923/grammophon acoustic sessions in berlin

bruno walter

beethoven coriolan overture

73   65928/69587
74

lp: deutsche grammophon 2740 259
cd: wing WCD 29/istituto discografico italiano IDIS 295-296

mendelssohn hebrides overture

82   65930/69589
83

lp: deutsche grammophon 2740 259
cd: istituto discografico italiano IDIS 295-296/deutsche grammophon 459 0002/459 0652

bizet carmen: preludes to acts three and four

1517   65954
1518

wagner a faust overture

1519   65955
71
72   65956

berlioz le carnaval romain overture

          69588/65929

cd: wing WCD 29

tchaikovsky symphony no 6: second movement

          69676

012/august-october 1923/grammophon acoustic sessions in berlin

leo blech

johann strauss perpetuum mobile; schubert-liszt march from d818
87   69578/65885
91

massenet scenes pittoresques
89   69579/65886
90
93   69580/65887
94

godard two movements from scenes poetiques
92   65888
95

rossini wilhelm tell overture
96   69582/65889
97
98   69583/65890
99

gounod marche funebre d'une marionette;
grieg holberg suite: prelude, sarabande and air
88   69593/65891
100
101   69594/65892
102

013/august-october 1923/grammophon acoustic session in berlin
hermann abendroth
johann strauss wiener blut waltz
108   69592/65875
109

014/august-october 1923/grammophon acoustic sessions in berlin
hans pfitzner
pfitzner die rose vom liebesgarten: truermarsch
221   65909/69628
222

pfitzner das käthchen von heilbronn: epilogue and march
223   65910/69629
224

pfitzner das christelflein overture
225   65869/69649
226

beethoven symphony no 7: abridged versions of second and fourth movements
227   66285/69648
228

weber der freischütz overture
229   65911/69620
230
231   65912/69621

014/august-october 1923/grammophon acoustic sessions in berlin/concluded

schumann symphony no 4 in d minor op 120

1406	66282/69625
1407	
1408	66283/69626
234	
232	66284/69627
233	

beethoven symphony no 6 in f op 68 "pastoral"

239	66254/69642
240	
241	66255/69643
235	
236	66256/69644
237	
238	66257/69645
1412	
1413	66258/69646
1414	
1415	66259/69647

beethoven symphony no 8: second movement

1405	66259/69647

pfitzner das fest auf solhaug: overture and act two finale

	65949
	65950

015/august-october 1923/grammophon acoustic session
otto marienhagen
mendelssohn meeresstille glückliche fahrt overture
259   69651/65952
260
261   69652/65953

016/august-october 1923/grammophon acoustic sessions
max von schillings
berlioz damnation de faust: danse des sylphes & marche hongroise
270   69654/65923   271

wagner parsifal: karfereitagszauber
272   69653/65922
273

wagner lohengrin act three prelude
311   69678/65959

017/august-october 1923/grammophon acoustic session
walter wohllebe
wagner parsifal prelude
308   69677/65958
309
310   69678/65959

018/august-october 1923/grammophon acoustic session in berlin

franz schreker

schreker der schatzgräber: zwischenspiel & nachtgesang

1313	69632/65924
1314	
1317	69633/65925
1318	
1319	69631/65912

019/august-october 1923/grammophon acoustic sessions in berlin

bruno seidler-winkler

josef strauss dorfschwalben aus österreich; johann strauss bei uns zu haus

1332	65957
1333	

saint-saens danse macabre

1448	69626/65927
1449	

020/august-october 1923/grammophon acoustic sessions in berlin
leo blech
mendelssohn ein sommernachtstraum: wedding march
1435   69652/65953

gluck iphigenie in aulis overture
1436   65893
1437

nicolai die lustigen weiber von windsor overture
1438   69623/65894
1439

mendelssohn ein sommernachtstraum: nocturne
2627   62465
2628

021/january 1924/grammophon acoustic session in berlin
leo blech
beethoven coriolan overture
      69624/65895

022/january 1924/grammophon acoustic sessions in berlin
rafaele benedito
granados goyescas intermezzo; albeniz suite espanola: granada
694   65973
695

albeniz suite espanola: sevillanas; cantos de espana: cordoba
696   65974
697

023/january 1924/grammophon acoustic session in berlin
hans pfitzner
weber preciosa overture
1527   65948
1528

024/january 1924/grammophon acoustic sessions in berlin
bruno seidler-winkler
weber der freischütz overture
        69634/65926

thomas raymonda overture
        65975

025/january 1924/grammophon acoustic sessions in berlin
otto marienhagen
wagner lohengrin prelude
        65951

wagner lohengrin act three prelude
        66046

026/1926/grammophon sessions in berlin using the pallophotophone (light-ray) system
hans pfitzner
schumann symphony no 4 in d minor op 120
80	66410
81	
82	66411
83	
84	66412
85	
86	66413

027/16 and 30 october 1926/grammophon sessions in berlin using the pallophotophone (light-ray) system
wilhelm furtwängler
weber der freischütz overture
172   66466
173
lp: japan JP 1101-1102/discocorp RR 431
cd: symposium 1043/dante LYS 116/koch 3-7059-2/japanese furtwängler society WFJ 18/WFJ 22/naxos 8.111003/andromeda ANDRCD 5008

beethoven symphony no 5 in c minor op 67
174   69855/brunswick 25005
175
216   69856/brunswick 25006
217
218   69857/brunswick 25007
179
330   69858/brunswick 25008
214
215   69859/brunswick 25009
lp: japan NA 122=123/discocorp RR 431/
british furtwängler society FURT 100
cd: koch 3-7059-2/japanese furtwängler society WFJ 18/japanese furtwängler centre WFHC 021-022/naxos 8.111003/
andromeda ANDRCD 5008
matrix 330 was recorded in early 1927; WFHC 021-022 contains versions of the symphony taken from both polydor and brunswick pressings

028/december 1926-october 1927/vox sessions in berlin
ernst kunwald
beethoven leonore no 3 overture
          08399
          08400

beethoven symphony no 7 in a op 92
1548   08430
1549
1550   08431
1559
1560   08432
1561
1562   08433
1563

liszt hungarian rhapsody no 2 in c sharp minor
          08546

029/1927/grammophon sessions in berlin hochschule für musik
julius prüwer
wagner rienzi overture
682   19815
683
684   19816

beethoven egmont overture
685   95281
686

030/1927-1928/grammophon sessions in berlin hochschule für musik

bruno kittel

beethoven missa solemnis op 123

with bruno-kittel-chor/emmy lund, soprano/lotte leonard, soprano/ elena schlosshauer-reynolds, contralto/anton maria topitz, tenor/ eugen transky, tenor/wilhelm guttmann, bass-baritone/ hermann schey, bass

655	95146
656	
657	95147
1162	
1163	95148
1164	
1169	95149
1170	
1171	95150
1176	
1177	95151
1178	
1212	95152
1213	
1214	95153
1221	
1222	95154
1223	
1230	95155
1231	
1232	95156

cd; deutsche grammophon (japan) POCG 60065-60066/ UCCG 90308-90309/459 5842

030/1927-1928/grammophon sessions in berlin/concluded
handel messiah: hallelujah chorus
with bruno-kittel-chor
658   66896

031/1927/grammophon session in berlin hochschule für musik
otto marienhagen
wagner lohengrin act three prelude
762   19816/27185/decca LY 6050

032/1927/grammophon sessions in berlin hochschule für musik
hans knappertsbusch
wagner die meistersinger von nürnberg overture
751   66698/cetra RR 8031/OR 5025/decca CA 8018
752
lp: deutsche grammophon LPEM 19 601/2740 259/heliodor 88 031
cd: preiser 90286/iron needle IN 1330/archiphon ARC 110-111/
deutsche grammophon 479 1148

wagner die meistersinger von nürnberg act three prelude
753   66780
754
lp: deutsche grammophon LPEM 19 601/heliodor 88 031
cd: preiser 90286/iron needle IN 1330/archiphon ARC 110-111/
grammofono AB 78678/urania URN 22127/
deutsche grammophon 479 1148

032/1927/grammophon sessions in berlin/continued
wagner tannhäuser: einzug der gäste
755   66702/27185/19862/brunswick 90299/decca LY 6047
lp: deutsche grammophon LPEM 19 078/heliodor 88 031
cd: preiser 90286/wing WCD 40/archiphon ARC 110-111/
urania URN 22127

wagner die meistersinger von nürnberg: tanz der lehrbuben
756   66705/66895
lp: deutsche grammophon LPEM 19 601/LPEM 19 078/heliodor 88 031
cd: preiser 90286/iron needle IN 1330/grammofono AB 78678/
urania URN 22127/archiphon ARC 110-111/
deutsche grammophon 479 1148

wagner parsifal: act one verwandlungsmusik
763   66700
764
lp: deutsche grammophon LPEM 19 601/2721 113/2740 259
cd: preiser 90286/iron needle IN 1330/archiphon ARC 110-111/
urania URN 22127/deutsche grammophon 479 1148

wagner die walküre: walkürenritt
765   66705/66895/cetra OR 5010/OR 5016/decca CA 8036
lp: deutsche grammophon LPEM 19 601/2740 259/heliodor 88 031
cd: preiser 90286/archiphon ARC 110-11/urania URN 22127/
deutsche grammophon 459 0012/459 0652/479 1148
matrix number 765 was replaced in 1939 by matrix number 1289

032/1927/grammophon sessions in berlin/concluded
wagner tannhäuser: venusberg music
766   66701/brunswick 90298
767
768   66702/brunswick 90299
lp: deutsche grammophon LPEM 19 601/2721 113/2740 259/ heliodor 88 031
cd: preiser 90286/iron needle IN 1330/grammofono AB 78678/ deutsche grammophon 479 1148

wagner der fliegende holländer overture
769   66830/cetra OR 5112
770
lp: deutsche grammophon LPEM 19 601
cd: preiser 90286/archiphon ARC 110-111/urania URN 22127

033/1927/grammophon sessions in berlin hochschule für musik
erich kleiber
schubert symphony no 8 in b minor D759 "unfinished"
773   66707
774
481   66708
776
777   66709
778
cd: berliner philharmoniker BPH 0603

034/1927/grammophon session in berlin hochschule für musik
oskar fried
stravinsky firebird suite
853   95052/516650/brunswick 90419/decca CA 8235
854
855   95053/516651/brunswick 90420/decca CA 8236
856
lp: deutsche grammophon 2721 070/2740 259/discocorp BWS 719
cd: dante LYS 386/koch 3-7146-2/arbiter 153/zyx PD 50252

035/1927/grammophon session in berlin hochschule für musik
alexander kitschin
tchaikovsky ouverture solennelle "1812"
with ural-kosaken-chor
857   95054/40226
858
859   95055/40227
860
cd: pristine audio PASC 268

036/10 november 1927/electrola sessions in berlin
hochschule für musik
leo blech
wagner tannhäuser: einzug der gäste; berlioz la damnation de faust: marche hongroise
CWR 1337   D 1498/EJ 216
CWR 1338

berlioz le carnaval romain overture
CWR 1339   D 1365/W 908
CWR 1340
cd: koch 3-7072-2

037/29-30 december 1927/grammophon sessions in berlin
hochschule für musik
bruno kittel
bach matthäus-passion: so ist mein jesus nun gefangen; wer hat dich so geschlagen?; o haupt voll blut und wunden; wir setzen uns mit tränen nieder
with bruno-kittel-chor/lotte leonard, soprano/emmi leisner, contralto
893   66720
894
895   66721
896

038/january-april 1928/grammophon sessions in berlin hochschule für musik

erich kleiber

mozart idomeneo overture; sechs deutsche tänze

1016	66729/brunswick 90106
489	
490	66730/brunswick 90107/decca CA 8171
491	

lp: deutsche grammophon LPEM 19 078 (K600 no 3 only)/
2740 259/rococo 2048 (K571 nos 4 and 6 and K600 no 3 only)

mendelssohn ein sommernachtstraum: scherzo and nocturne

972	66731
973	
974	66850

lp: deutsche grammophon 2721 070/2740 259
cd: zyx music PD 5042 (nocturne only)

039/february 1928/vox session in berlin

ernst kunwald

beethoven coriolan overture

1724	08559
1725	

040/february 1928/grammophon sessions in berlin
hochschule für musik
franz schreker
bizet l'arlesienne: suite no 1
15   66703/27237
18
17   66704/27238
18.
19   66801/27241

041/february-april 1928/grammophon sessions in berlin
hochschule für musik
hans pfitzner
weber oberon overture
917   95091/brunswick 90042/decca CA 8015
918

mendelssohn hebrides overture
919   27292/decca CA 6093
920
lp: deutsche grammophon 2740 259

weber jubel overture
921   19858
922

042/april-september 1928/grammophon sessions in berlin hochschule für musik
jascha horenstein
bruckner symphony no 7 in e
964	66802/brunswick 90305
965	
966	66803/brunswick 90306
967	
1270	66804/brunswick 90307
1271	
1272	66805/brunswick 90308
1273	
1274	66806/brunswick 90309
1275	
1330	66807/brunswick 90310
1331	
1332	66808/brunswick 90311
1333	

lp: unicorn UNI 111
cd: koch 3-7022-2/pristine PASC 203/
berliner philharmoniker BPH 0602

043/april-september 1928/grammophon sessions in berlin hochschule für musik
alexander kitschin
glazunov stenka rasin
968	95088
969	
970	95089
971	

cd: pristine audio PASC 268

044/september-october 1928/grammophon sessions in berlin hochschule für musik

julius prüwer

liszt piano concerto no 1 in e flat
with alexander brailowsky, piano
993   66750
994
995   66751
996
997   66752
cd: danacord DACOCD 338-339

chopin piano concerto no 1 in e minor
with alexander brailowsky, piano
1003   66753/67470
1004
1005   66754/67471
1006
1007   66755/67472
1008
1009   66756/67473
1010
cd: danacord DACOCD 336-337

lortzing der waffenschmied overture
1172   19901
1173

johann strauss der zigeunerbaron overture
1174   19902/15130
1175

044/september-october 1928/grammophon sessions in berlin/concluded

meyerbeer les huguenots overture
1180   19898
1181

donizetti la fille du regiment overture
1182   19899
1183

flotow alessandro stradella overture
1184   19900
1185

suppe die schöne galathea overture
1215   19903/15155
1216

gluck iphigenie in aulis overture
1217   19904
1218

mendelssohn hebrides overture
1219   19905
1220

045/september-october 1928/grammophon sessions in berlin hochschule für musik
albert wolff
lalo le roi d'ys overture; bizet carmen prelude
1021	66722/35045
1022	
1023	66723/35046
1024	

falla la vida breve: interlude and danza
1025	66724
1026	

faure pelleas et melisande suite; ravel pavane pour une infante defunte
1027	66725
1028	
1029	66726
1030	

sicilienne from pelleas et melisande and carmen prelude also coupled together on 66727/35047

046/october 1928/grammophon session in berlin hochschule für musik
max roth
vladigeroff bulgarian rhapsody
1046	95090/decca CA 8147
1047	

047/6-13 october 1928/grammophon sessions in berlin hochschule für musik

oskar fried

liszt mazeppa

1267   66787/brunswick 90165/decca CA 8177
1268
1269   66788/brunswick 90166/decca CA 8178
1340
lp: discocorp BWS 734
cd: koch 3-7146-2/music and arts CD 1185

liszt les preludes

1341   66812/brunswick 90163/decca CA 8166
1342
1343   66813/brunswick 90164/decca CA 8167
1344
cd: koch 3-7146-2/music and arts CD 1185

weber euryanthe overture

205   19988
206
lp: deutsche grammophon 2740 259
cd: music and arts CD 1198

grieg peer gynt: suites one and two

         95033/516608
         95034/516609
         95035/516610
         95036/516611

047/6-13 october 1928/grammophon sessions in berlin hochschule für musik/concluded

rimsky-korsakov scheherazade

1359	95187/brunswick 90361
1360	
1361	95188/brunswick 90362
1362	
1363	95189/brunswick 90363
1364	
1365	95190/brunswick 90364
1363	
1387	95191/brunswick 90365
1388	
1389	95192/brunswick 90366

cd: koch 3-7146-2/dante LYS 386

fried fantasy on humperdinck's hänsel und gretel

1416	19984
1417	
1418	19985
1419	

cd: music and arts CD 1167

saint-saens danse macabre

1420	95204/92094
1421	

lp: deutsche grammophon 2740 259
cd: dante LYS 280/arbiter 153

048/18 october 1928/grammophon session in berlin hochschule für musik
kurt atterberg
atterberg symphony no 6 in c
1424   95193
1425
1426   95194
1427
1428   95195
1429

049/october-december 1928/grammophon sssions in berlin hochschule für musik
julius prüwer
berlioz benvenuto cellini overture; la damnation de faust: marche hongroise
1282   95252
1284
1285   95253
1286

meyerbeer le prophete: coronation march
1283   95211/95254

049/october-december 1928/grammophon sessions in berlin hochschule für musik/concluded

schubert symphony no 8 in b minor D759 "unfinished"

1313	66784
1314	
1315	66785
1316	
1317	66786
1318	

johann strauss frühlingsstimmen waltz

1319	19860

johann strauss kaiserwalzer

1336	19949
1337	

johann strauss liebeslieder-walzer

1338	19950
1339	

brahms academic festival overture

1408	95210
1409	
1410	95211

050/october 1928/grammophon session in berlin hochschule für musik
felix lederer
bizet carmen: the four preludes
218   19989/21893
219

051/december 1928/grammophon session in berlin hochschule für musik
franz schreker
bizet l'arlesienne suite no 2
1334   66799
1335
1336   66800
1356
1357   66801

052/6, 10 and 17 december 1928/grammophon sessions in berlin hochschule für musik

richard strauss
cornelius der barbier von bagdad overture
1496   66936
1497
lp: deutsche grammophon 2548 736
cd: koch 3-7119-2/documents 232 597/dutton CDBP 9785/ deutsche grammophon 479 2703

weber euryanthe overture
1498   66828
1499
lp: deutsche grammophon 2548 736
cd: koch 3-7119-2/documents 232 597/dutton CDBP 9785/ deutsche grammophon 479 2703

gluck iphigenie in aulis overture, arranged by wagner
1500   66829/516625/brunswick 90110
1501
lp: deutsche grammophon 2548 736/2740 259
cd: koch 3-7119-2/documents 232 597/dutton CDBP 9785/ deutsche grammophon 479 2703

wagner der fliegende holländer overture
1506   66830/brunswick 90120
1507
lp: deutsche grammophon 2548 736/2721 113
cd: koch 3-7119-2/documents 232 597/dutton CDBP 9785/ deutsche grammophon 479 2703

052/december 1928/grammophon sessions/concluded
wagner lohengrin prelude
1508   unpublished
1509

wagner tristan prelude with concert ending
1510   66832
1511
lp: deutsche grammophon 2548 736
cd: koch 3-7119-2/documents 232 597/dutton CDBP 9785/
deutsche grammophon 479 2703

strauss salome: tanz der sieben schleier
1520   66827/brunswick 90088/fonit 91020/decca CA 8017
1521
45: deutsche grammophon EPL 30 538
lp: rococo 2015/first editions FER 1/deutsche grammophon
2548 722/2740 160/2740 259
cd: koch 3-7119-2/deutsche grammophon 479 2703
rococo edition incorrectly described orchestra as berlin staatskapelle

053/january 1929/grammophon sessions in berlin hochschule für musik

manfred gurlitt

beethoven violin concerto in d op 61

with josef wolfsthal, violin

1534	95243
1535	
1536	95244
1537	
1538	95245
1547	
1548	95246
1549	
1550	95247
1551	

lp: deutsche grammophon 2721 070

cd: pearl GEMMCD 9387/deutsche grammophon 453 8042/ symposium 1141

054/january 1929/grammophon sessions in berlin
hochschule für musik

julius prüwer

meyerbeer fackeltanz no 1
1570   27038
1571

rubinstein toreador et andalouse
1572   95254

thomas raymonda overture
1573   27058
1574

brahms hungarian dances no 5 and 6
1602   21643
1603

055/january-june 1929/grammophon sessions in berlin
hochschule für musik
julius kopsch
beethoven fidelio overture
241   27038
242

smetana bartered bride overture
243   27034
244

berlioz beatrice et benedict overture
901   27163/15018
902

056/january-june 1929/grammophon sessions in berlin
hochschule für musik
jascha horenstein
bach chorale preludes arranged by schoenberg: komm gott schöpfer; schmücke dich o liebe seele!
799   95295
800
cd: koch 3-7054-2

057/13 june 1929/grammophon sessions in berlin hochschule für musik
wilhelm furtwängler
mendelssohn ein sommernachtstraum overture
857   66925/69206/brunswick 90137
858
859   66926/69207/brunswick 90138
lp: heliodor 88 021/deutsche grammophon 2535 821
cd: dante LYS 116/documents 20 3090/20 3093/223 508/koch 3-7073-2/ french furtwängler society SWF 042-044/anfromeda ANDRCD 5008/ naxos 8.111004

bach air from orchestral suite no 3
860   66926/66935/95418/brunswick 90050/decca CA 8014
45: deutsche grammophon EPL 30 164
lp: deutsche grammophon LPEM 19 078/2535 827/japan JP 1101-1102
cd: music and arts CD 954/koch 3-7059-2/documents 223 508/ french furtwängler society SWF 042-044/andromeda ANDRCD 5008/ japanese furtwängler society WFJ 15-16/naxos 8.111136

schubert ballet music no 2 from rosamunde incidental music
861   66935/95458/brunswick 90050/decca CA 8098
45: deutsche grammophon EPL 30 164
lp: heliodor 88 021/deutsche grammophon 2721 070
cd: symposium 1043/palladio PD 4176/dante LYS 114/documents 20 3090/20 393/223 508/koch 3-7059-2/andromeda ANDRCD 5008/ french furtwängler society SWF 042-044/naxos 8.111136/ deutsche grammophon 477 5238

057/13 june 1929/grammophon sessions in berlin/concluded
schubert entr'acte no 3 from rosamunde incidental music
862   95418/95458/brunswick 90162/decca CA 8098
lp: heliodor 88 021/japan AT 05-06/deutsche grammophon 2721 070
cd: symposium 1043/palladio PD 4176/dante LYS 114/documents 20 3090/20 3093/223 508/koch 3-7059-2/andromeda ANDRCD 5008/ french furtwängler society SWF 042-044/naxos 8.111136
matrix number 862 was re-dubbed for some issues as 1102, leading to the incorrect assumption that these were two separate recordings

058/1929/grammophon sessions in berlin hochschule
für musik
hans pfitzner
beethoven symphony no 3 in e flat op 55 "eroica"
917	66939/brunswick 90060/decca CA 8047
918	
919	66940/brunswick 90061/decca CA 8048
920	
921	66941/brunswick 90062/decca CA 8049
922	
923	66942/brunswick 90063/decca CA 8050
924	
925	66943/brunswick 90064/decca CA 8051
926	
203	66944/brunswick 90065/decca CA 8052
928	

cd: preiser 90201/naxos 8.110910

059/1929/grammophon sessions in berlin schumannsaal
jascha horenstein
haydn symphony no 94 in g "surprise"
132	66914/15068
133	
134	66915/15069
135	
136	66916/15070
137	

cd: koch 3-7054-2

mozart le nozze di figaro overture; la clemenza di tito overture
138	95296
139	

schubert symphony no 5 in b flat d485
140	66932/95402
141	
142	66933/95403
150	
151	66934/95404

according to michael gray the conductor was not named on the original issues of the mozart and schubert items

060/12 august 1929/grammophon session in berlin hochschule für musik
wilhelm furtwängler
brahms hungarian dance no 3 in f
1648   unpublished
1649
cd: japanese furtwängler society WFJ 18
according to rene tremine this ten-inch disc was discovered as recently as 1995 and was incorrectly labelled as hungarian dance no 1

061/september-november 1929/ultraphon sessions in berlin wilhelmsaue studios
carl schuricht
weber der freischütz overture
30353   E 265/clangor MD 69/decca K 460
30354

tchaikovsky capriccio italien
30355   E 264/clangor MD 1573
30356

bixet l'arlesienne suite no 1
30357   E 285/E 1850
30358
30359   E 286/E 1851
30360

offenbach orphee aux enfers overture
30361   E 120
30362
cd: iron needle IN 1393/dante LYS 180

062/27 september 1929/ultraphon session in berlin wilhelmsaue studios

wilhelm grosz

suppe die schöne galathea overture
30289   E 192
30290

063/24 october 1929/ultraphon session in berlin wilhelmsaue studios

fritz zweig

meyerbeer les huguenots: une dame noble; verdi un ballo in maschera: saper vorreste
with tilly de garmo, soprano
10389   A 425
10390

064/13 december 1929/ultraphon sessions in berlin wilhelmsaue studios
selmar meyrowitz
bizet carmen: la fleur que tu m'avais jetee; puccini la boheme: che gelida manina
with louis graveure, tenor
30382   F 310
30383
lp: discophilia KG-9-2

wagner tannhäuser: wohl wusst ich hier sie im gebet zu finden; o du mein holder abendstern
with herbert janssen, baritone
30384   E 311
30385
lp: telefunken 6.42332
cd: teldec 8573 830222

wagner lohengrin: atmest du nicht mit mir die süssen düfte?; in fernem land
with louis graveure, tenor
30386   F 312
30387

065/6 january, 7 february and 5 june 1930/grammophon sessions in berlin hochschule für musik

wilhelm furtwängler

wagner lohengrin prelude

1085   95408/91030/brunswick 90231/decca CA 8089
1086
lp: heliodor 88 021/top classic TC 9054
cd: documents 20 3090/20 3092/223 508/koch 3-7073-2/french furtwängler society SWF 042-044/andromeda ANDRCD 5008/ naxos 8.111005/archipel ARPCD 0261

wagner tristan prelude und liebestod

1087   95438/91028/brunswick 90201/decca CA 8039
1088
1089   95439/91029/brunswick 90202/decca CA 8156
1090
45: deutsche grammophon EPL 30 540 (liebestod only)
lp: heliodor 88 021
cd: koch 3-7073-2/french furtwängler society SWF 042-044/ naxos 8.111005/andromeda ANDRCD 5008

schubert rosamunde overture d644

1091   brunswick 90147
1092
lp: british furtwängler society FURT 100/japan JP 1101-1102/AT 05-06
cd: symposium 1043/palladio PD 4176/dante LYS 114/documents 20 3090/20 3092/223 508/french furtwängler society SWF 042-044/ koch 3-7059-2/naxos 8.111136/andromeda ANDRCD 5008

065/january-june 1930/grammophon sessions in berlin/continued

strauss till eulenspiegels lustige streiche: rehearsal sequence
1093   unpublished
1094
lp: deutsche grammophon 2740 260/japan AT 13-14/
french furtwängler society SWF 7906
cd: french furtwängler society SWF 042-044

strauss till eulenspiegels lustige streiche
1095   95410/91024/decca CA 8053
1096
1097   95411/91025/decca CA 8054
lp: rococo 2014/japan JP 1101-1102/deutsche grammophon 2740 260
cd: arlecchino ARL 111-112/documents 20 3090/20 3093/223 508/
koch 3-7073-2/french furtwängler society SWF 042-044/
naxos 8.111005/andromeda ANDRCD 5008

mendelssohn hebrides overture
1098   95470/brunswick 90401/decca CA 8090
1099
lp: heliodor 88 021/deutsche grammophon 2535 821
cd: grammofono AB 78574/dante LYS 116/koch 3-7073-2/deutsche grammophon 477 5238/french furtwängler society SWF 042-044/
naxos 8.111004/japanese furtwängler society WFFC 1406/
andromeda ANDRCD 5008

mendelssohn hebrides overture: rehearsal sequence
1100   unpublished
cd: tahra FURT 1008-1011/french furtwängler society SWF 042-044/
deutsche grammophon 477 5238

065/january-june 1930/grammophon sessions in berlin/continued

berlioz la damnation de faust: marche hongroise
1101   95411/91025/decca CA 8054
lp: heliodor 88 021
cd: koch 3-7073-2/french furtwängler society SWF 042-044/naxos 8.111004/japanese furtwängler society WFJ 15-16/ andromeda ANDRCD 5008

dvorak slavonic dance op 46 no 3
1103   unpublished
cd: tahra FURT 1008-1011/french furtwängler society SWF 042-044/ deutsche grammophon 477 5238

bach brandenburg concerto no 3 in g bwv1048
1104   95417/brunswick 90161/decca CA 8013
1105
1106   95418/brunswick 90162/decca CA 8014
45: deutsche grammophon EPL 30 539
lp: deutsche grammophon 2535 827/discocorp RR 431
cd: symposium 1043/grammofono AB 78574/dante LYS 117/ music and arts CD 954/documents 20 3090/20 3093/223 508/ koch 3-7059-2/french furtwängler society SWF 042-044/ naxos 8.111136/japanese furtwängler society WFJ 15-16/ andromeda ANDRCD 5008

065/january-june 1930/grammophon sessions in berlin/concluded
rossini la gazza ladra overture
1108   95427/91021/brunswick 90188/decca CA 8055
1109
lp: heliodor 88 021/japan AT 13-14
cd: grammofono AB 78574/dante LYS 116/music and arts CD 954/ documents 20 3090/20 393/223 508/koch 3-7059-2/french furtwängler society SWF 042-044/naxos 8.111003/andromeda ANDRCD 5008/ japanese furtwängler society WFJ 15-16

brahms hungarian dances nos 1 and 10
2580   90109/brunswick 85034/decca DE 7008
2587
lp: heliodor 88 021/melodiya D 030275-030276
cd: symposium 1043/dante LYS 204/koch 3-7073-2/documents 223 508/ deutsche grammophon 477 5238/french furtwängler society SWF 042-044/ naxos 8.111005/japanese furtwängler society WFJ 15-16/ andromeda ANDRCD 5008

066/january 1930/grammophon session in berlin
alois melichar
hruby potpourri aus wiener-meister-operetten
1226   27280
1227

067/8 january 1930/ultraphon session in berlin wilhelmsaue studios
selmar meyrowitz/*wilhelm grosz
lortzing der wildschütz: fünftausend taler!
with leo schützendorf, bass-baritone
30388   E 725
cd: preiser 89186

lortzing zar und zimmermann: o sancta justitia!
with leo schützendorf, bass-baritone
30389   E 221
30390
cd: preiser 89186

*weinberger potpourri on themes from schwanda der dudelsackpfeifer
30391   E 299
30392

068/13 january 1930/ultraphon session in berlin wilhelmsaue studios
carl schuricht
wagner der fliegende holländer overture
30395   E 331/clangor MD 59
30396
cd: iron needle IN 1393/dante LYS 147

069/10 february 1930/ultraphon sessions in berlin wilhelmsaue studios
selmar meyrowitz/*theo mackeben
*potpourri on themes from smetana's bartered bride
30412   E 358
30413

wagner die meistersinger von nürnberg: am stillen herd; morgenlich leuchtend
with paul kötter, tenor
30414   E 359
30415
lp: telefunken HT 46
cd: preiser 89975

puccini la boheme: si mi chiamano mimi; tosca: vissi d'arte
with elisabeth grünwald, soprano/*sung in german*
30416   E 360
30417

puccini la boheme act three prelude
30418   E 472/E 706

verdi la forza del destino: solenne in quest' ors; otello: si per ciel
with paul schöffler, bass-baritone/*sung in german*
30419   E 361
30420
cd: preiser 89975

070/14 february 1930/columbia sessions in berlin beethovensaal

bruno walter

strauss salome: tanz der sieben schleier
WAX 5444   LX 39/DWX 1342/GQX 10705/67814D
WAX 5445
lp: emi RLS 768/1C137 54095-54099
cd: emi 300 0122

strauss der rosenkavalier: act three waltzes
WAX 5446   LX 60/DWX 1348/LFX 94/67892D
WAX 5447
lp: emi RLS 768/1C137 54095-54099
cd: emi 300 0122

johann strauss rosen aus dem süden waltz
WAX 5448   LX 28/DWX 1337/GQX 10989/M 364
WAX 5449
cd: dante LYS 358/preiser 90090

071/28 february 1930/ultraphon session in berlin
wilhelmsaue studios
selmar meyrowitz/*wilhelm grosz
*mozart eine kleine nachtmusik k525
30429	E 393/clangor MD 9249
30430	
30431	E 394/clangor MD 9250
30432	

rimsky-korsakov le coq d'or: hymne au soleil
with xenia belmas, soprano
30433   F 395
lp: club 99 99-13
cd: preiser 89513
russian and french versions of the aria were recorded, both using same matrix number

072/28 march 1930/concert recording in hamburg musikhalle
wilhelm furtwängler
hindemith konzertmusik
unpublished recording of the world premiere performance

073/3 april 1930/ultraphon sessions in berlin wilhelmsaue studios
theo mackeben/*fritz zweig
orchestral fantasy on verdi's la traviata
30445   E 503
30446

orchestral fantasy on zeller's der vogelhändler
30447   E 443
30448

*mozart symphony no 39: third movement
30449   E 442

074/11 april 1930/ultraphon session in berlin wilhelmsaue studios
erich kleiber
bach-schoenberg prelude and fugue bwv552
30458   E 463
30459
30460   E 464
cd: preiser 90311

075/14 april 1930/ultraphon sessions in berlin wilhelmsaue studios
selmar meyrowitz/*ernst viebig
*albeniz suite espanola: granada and cataluna
30463   E 343/E 849

borodin prince igor: polovtsian dances
30464   E 452
30465

johann strauss morgenblätter waltz
30466   E 691

wagner die walküre: walkürenritt
10881   A 473/clangor MD 67
10882

076/15 april 1930/ultraphon sessions in berlin wilhelmsaue studios
alexander von zemlinsky/*ernst viebig
smetana ma vlast: the moldau; weinberger schwanda der dudelsackpfeiffer: polka
30467   E 465
30468
30469   E 466
30470
cd: koch 11401/310 037 (smetana)

*grosses johann-strauss-potpourri
30471   E 467
30472

077/5 june 1930/ultraphon sessions in berlin wilhelmsaue studios
selmar meyrowitz/*theo mackeben
boccherini menuetto and canzonetta
11017   A 539
11020

schubert moment musical no 3; sarasate danza espanola
11021   A 540
11022

***scassola suite pastorale**
11023   A 541
11024

***grothe russische fantasie**
11025   A 521
11026

078/16 june 1930/concert recording in philharmonie
wilhelm furtwängler
beethoven symphony no 9: second movement
unpublished recording with tape nuber RRG 937-937

079/17 june 1930/ultraphon session in berlin wilhelmsaue studios
erich kleiber
berlioz benvenuto cellini overture; la damnation de faust: marche hongroise
30489   E 532
30490
30491   E 533
30492
cd: teldec 3984 284072 (overture only)

080/18-19 june 1930/ultraphon sessions in berlin wilhelmsaue studios
selmar meyrowitz
puccini tosca: te deum and tre sbirri
with wilhelm rode, baritone/*sung in german*
30493   F 527
30494
lp: preiser LV 17/discophilia KGR 3

verdi aida: ciel mio padre!
with eva hadrabova, soprano & wilhelm rode, baritone/
sung in german
30495   F 535
30496
lp: preiser LV 17/discophilia KGR 3/telefunken HT 47

080/18-19 june 1930/ultraphon sessions in berlin/concluded
boito mefistofele: son lo spirito che nega
with wilhelm rode, bass-baritone/*sung in german*
30497   F 525
lp: preiser LV 17/discophilia KGR 3/telefunken HT 47

meyerbeer l'africaine: re dell' onde profonde
with wilhelm rode, bass-baritone/*sung in german*
30498   F 534
lp: preiser LV 17/discophilia KGR 3

borodin prince igor: no rest no sleep
with alexander krajeff, tenor
30499   E 536
30500

rubinstein nero: arie des vindex
with alexander krajeff, tenor
11041   A 739

081/21 august 1930/ultraphon sessions in berlin wilhelmsaue studios

ernst viebig

fantasy on wagner's meistersinger
15069   E 650
15070

josef strauss dorfschwalben aus österreich; johann strauss rosen aus dem süden
15071   A 567
15072

johann strauss kaiserwalzer
15073   A 568
15074

fantasy on abraham's viktoria und ihr husar
15075   E 572
15076

082/11-13 september 1930/ultraphon sessions in berlin wilhelmsaue studios

erich kleiber

strauss till eulenspiegels lustige streiche
15166   E 651
15167
15168   E 652
15169
cd: preiser 90311/musica classica 2003-2004/
berliner philharmoniker BPH 0603

beethoven coriolan overture
15170   E 653/E 22284
15171
cd: doremi DHR 7752/teldec 3984 284072

wagner götterdämmerung: siegfrieds trauermarsch
15172   E 612
15173

dvorak scherzo capriccioso
15179   E 655
15180
cd: naxos 8.110907

janacek lachian dance no 1
15181   E 598/E 938/E 1052
cd: preiser 90311

083/12 september 1930/ultraphon sessions in berlin
wilhelmsaue studios
selmar meyrowitz
wagner die walküre: winterstürme wichen dem wonnemond;
siegmund heiss ich!
with paul kötter, tenor
15174   E 654
15175
lp: telefunken 6.42332 (winterstürme)
cd: preiser 89975

wagner götterdämmerung: siegfrieds rheinfahrt
15176   unpublished

kienzl der evangelimann: selig sind die verfolgung leiden;
lortzing zar und zimmermann: leb wohl mein flandrisch mädchen!
with paul kötter, tenor
15177   A 661
15178
cd: preiser 89975 (evangelimann)

084/16 september 1930/ultraphon session in berlin
wilhelmsaue studios
carl schuricht
weber oberon overture
15198   E 656
15199
lp: royale 513

085/17 september 1930/ultraphon session in berlin
wilhelmsaue studios
wilhelm grosz
kalman fortissimo
15211   E 657
15212

johann strauss annen polka
15213   A 740

johann strauss seid umschlungen walzer
15214   E 691

086/september-october 1930/ultraphon session in berlin
wilhelmsaue studio
unnamed conductor
weihnachtslieder: o du fröhliche; stille nacht
with ursula van diemen, soprano
15360   A 619
15361

087/10-24 october 1930/ultraphon sessions in berlin wilhelmsaue studios

selmar meyrowitz

mozart der schauspieldiretor overture; 3 deutsche tänze
15435   E 741
15481

mozart le nozze di figaro: non piu andrai
with leo schützendorf, bass-baritone/*sung in german*
15436   E 725

potpourri of themes by puccini
15439   E 704
15440

wagner tannhäuser overture
15441   E 705/clangor MD 61
15442
15443   E 706/clangor MD 63

potpourri of themes by lortzing
15484   A 726
15485

088/24 october-4 december 1930/ultraphon sssions in berlin wilhelmsaue studios

wilhelm grosz

johann strauss g'schichten aus dem wienerwald
15486   A 727
15487

088/october-december 1930/ultraphon sessions/concluded
godard mazurka; rubinstein valse caprice
15899   A 734/clangor MD 155/royale 1728
15900

niederberger ich liebe dich
with joseph schmidt, tenor
15601   A 764
coupled with 15971 (session no. 090)

089/8 december 1930/ultraphon sessions in berlin wilhelmsaue studios
selmar meyrowitz
weber der freischütz: hier im irdishen jammertal; schweig einmal still
with michael bohnen, bass
15910   F 738
15911

verdi rigoletto: la donna e mobile; questa o quella
with joseph schmidt, tenor/*sung in german*
15912   A 779
15913
lp: telefunken HT 10/TH 97007

flotow alessandro stradella overture
15914   A 780
15915

090/18 december 1930/ultraphon sessions in berlin wilhelmsaue studios
erich orthmann/*wilhelm grosz
georg: liebling nach dem tango; vergiss mein nicht!
with joseph schmidt, tenor
15971   A 764
coupled with 15601 (session no. 088)

*rachmaninov prelude in c sharp minor; liszt liebestraum in e flat
15972   A 816/clangor MD 1559
15973

091/18-19 december 1930/ultraphon sessions in berlin wilhelmsaue studios
selmar meyrowitz/*hans schlager
potpourri of themes by mozart
15974   E 817/clangor MD 73
15975

*potpourri of themes from lehar's schön ist die welt
15961   A 763
15963

092/1931/newsreel footage in berlin philharmonie
bruno walter
weber oberon overture
dvd: dreamlife (japan) DLVC 1009

093/1931/grammophon sessions in berlin hochschule für musik

max fiedler

brahms symphony no 2 in d op 73

1162	95453/27254/decca CA 8004
1163	
1164	95454/27255/decca CA 8005
1165	
1166	95455/27256/decca CA 8006
1167	
1168	95456/27257/decca CA 8007
1169	
1170	95457/27258/decca CA 8008

lp: deusche grammophon 2721 070
cd: biddulph WHL 003-004

brahms academic festival overture

1171	27271/decca LY 6058
1172	

cd: biddulph WHL 003-004/pristine audio PASC 363

094/1931/grammophon sessions in berlin hochschule für musik
alois melichar/*franz schreker
johann strauss o schöner mai waltz
3022   24364
3023

*schreker kleine suite
3073   24972
3074
3083   24973
3085

095/12 january and 9 february 1931/ultraphon sessions in berlin wilhelmsaue studios
erich kleiber
berlioz symphonie fantastique: valse
16028   E 808
16029

gluck iphigenie in aulis overture
16030   E 844
16031

strauss der rosenkavalier: act three waltzes
16181   E 853
16182
cd: preiser 90311

096/12-27 january 1931/ultraphon sessions in berlin wilhelmsaue studios
selmar meyrowitz
handel dank sei dir herr; giulio cesare: v'adoro pupille
with eva lindenberg, contralto/*sung in german*
16032   E 807
16033
lp: preiser LV 134

potpourri of themes from verdi operas
16036   E 805/clangor MD 77
16037
16038   E 806/clangor MD 79
16039

herold zampa overture
16214   E 926/clangor MD 81
16215

097/9-23 february 1930/ultraphon sessions in berlin wilhelmsaue studios
selmar meyrowitz
wagner die meistersinger von nürnberg overture
16183   E 854/clangor MD 65
16184

moszowski spanish dances
16222   E 840

097/february 1931/ultrphon sessions in berlin/concluded

rossini la gazza ladra overture

16216   E 991
16217

auber fra diavolo overture

16218   E 1018
16219

potpourri of themes from puccini operas

16220   E 878
16221

verdi rigoletto: questo o quella

with joseph schmidt, tenor
16223   A 779
lp: telefunken HT 10/TH 97007
cd: teldec 0927 426652

potpourri of themes from old operas

16243   A 879/clangor MD 87
16244

098/19 march 1931/ultraphon session in berlin wilhelmsaue studios

theo mackeben

potpourri of themes from offenbach operettas
16456   A 888
16457

mendelssohn frühlingslied; paderewski minuet in g
16458   A 889
16459

099/26 march 1931/ultraphon session in berlin wilhelmsaue studios

wilhelm grosz

lanner hofballtänze; josef strauss sphärenklänge waltz
16567   A 928
16569

johann strauss frühlingsstimmen waltz; lagunenwalzer
16568   A 1020
16570

100/4-16 april 1931/ultraphon sessions in berlin wilhelmsaue studios

selmar meyrowitz
potpourri of themes by chopin
16616   A 992
16617

verdi un ballo in maschera: re dell' abisso; thomas mignon: connais-tu le pays?
with eugenia heilbrun, contralto/*sung in german*
16630   E 999
16632

brüll das goldene kreuz: wo anders?; nessler der trompeter von säckingen: behüt dich gott
with cornelis bronsgeest, baritone
16635   A 980
16636

potpourri of themes by grieg
16637   E 929
16638

beethoven adagio from moonlight sonata; adagio from piano sonata op 27 no 1
15898   E 801
16639

chopin funeral march; beethoven funeral march
16640   A 1019
16641

101/9 june 1931/ultraphon session in berlin wilhelmsaue studios
selmar meyrowitz
potpourri of themes from bizet's carmen
17011   E 965
17012

wagner rienzi overture
17013   E 962
17014

102/10-13 june 1931/ultraphon sessions in berlin bachsaal
erich kleiber
johann strauss kaiserwalzer
17015   E 964/clangor MD 1033
17016
cd: preiser 90395/biddulph WHL 002/teldec 4509 955132/ 3984 284112/archiphon ARC 102

johann strauss an der schönen blauen donau
17017   E 963
17018
cd: preiser 90395/tahra TAH 358-361/teldec 4509 951132/ 3984 284112

beethoven egmont overture
17019   E 961
17020
cd: teldec 3984 269192

102/june 1931/ultraphon sessions in berlin/concluded
smetana the bartered bride overture
17021   E 1017
17022

weber-berlioz aufforderung zum tanz
17033   E 988
17034
cd: biddulph WHL 002/archiphon ARC 102

lanner schönbrunnerwalzer
17035   E 990
17036
cd: teldec 4509 955132/3984 284072

dvorak holubka: wedding dance
17037   E 1052

103/15-16 june 1931/grammophon sessions in berlin hochschule für musik (15 june) and lützowstrasse studio (16 june)
alois melichar
offenbach orfee aux enfers overture
2658   24233
2659

strauss schlagobers: waltz and march
634   27300
635

104/1931/kristall sessions in berlin
clemens schmalstich
fantasy on themes from mascagni's cavalleria rusticana
C032   1029
C033

fantasy on themes from puccini's la boheme
C034   1030
C035

fantasy on themes from leoncavallo's i pagliacci
C036   1031
C037

fantasy on themes from puccini's madama butterfly
C038   1032
C039

potpourri of waltzes by johann strauss
C044   1039
C045

105/1932/grammophon sessions in berlin lützowstrasse studio
alois melichar
bach brandenburg concerto no 2 in f bwv1047
with szymon goldberg, violin/paul sporri, trumpet/albert harzer, flute/gustav bora, oboe/hans bottemund, cello/
eigel kruttye, harpsichord
1251   27293/15236/decca LY 6061
1252
1253   27294/15237/decca LY 6062
1254
cd: music and arts CD 1225

fantasy on themes by grieg
5113   25061
5114

106/1932/grammophon sessions in berlin lützowstrasse studio
hans pfitzner
pfitzner das herz: liebesmelodie
5292   25273
5293
lp: heliodor 88 014
cd: deutsche grammophon 459 0652
matrix numbers 5292 and 5293 were replaced in 1939 by 3678 and 3679

lanner pestherwalzer
5294   25274/10133
5295
cd: pristine audio PASC 305

107/1932/grammophon session in berlin hochschule für musik
franz schreker
grieg peer gynt suite no 1
3086   24627
3087
3088   24628
3089

108/1932/grammophon sessions in berlin lützowstrasse studio and *hochschule für musik
alois melichar
luigini ballet egyptien
3120   24638
3121
3122   24639
3123

fantasy on themes from wagner's die meistersinger von nürnberg
3142   24800/10001
3143

*ippollitov-ivanov caucasian sketches: procession of the sardar; rimsky-korsakov tsar sultan: flight of the bumble bee
3173   25027/10230
5064

108/1932/grammophon sessions in berlin/concluded
massenet scenes pittoresques
3211   24930
3212
3213   24931
3214

delibes sylvia ballet suite
3307   24960/10092
3308
3309   24961/10093
3310
3311   24962/10094
3312

popy ballet suite
1211   27288
1212

109/25 january 1932/ultraphon sessions in berlin
wilhelmsaue studio
hans schleger
fantasy on themes from old operettas
18210 A 1057
18211

suppe morgen mittag und abend in wien overture
18212 A 1058
18213

waldteufel espana; estudianita
18214 A 1059
18215

ivanovici donauwellenwalzer; johann strauss liebesliederwalzer
18216 A 1060
18217

110/17 february 1932/ultraphon sessions in berlin singakademie
selmar meyrowitz/*leo blech
wagner lohengrin prelude
18237   E 1053
18238
18238 was recorded on 5 april 1932

mascagni cavalleria rusticana intermezzo; leoncavallo
i pagliacci intermezzo
18239   E 1054
18240

*bizet carmen ballet suite; smetana bartered bride polka
18241   E 1055
18302

wagner kaisermarsch
18261   E 1084
18262

*mendelssohn ein sommernachtstraum: wedding march;
meyerbeer le prophete: coronation march
18303   E 1056
18301

111/7 march 1932/telefunken sessions in berlin wilhelmsaue studio

hans schleger

hildebrandt eine walzer-redoute
18270   A 1087
18271

translateur engellied; was blumen träumen
18272   unpublished
18273

van heykens ständchen; cremieux quand l'amour meurt valse
18274   A 1091
18275

112/15 march 1932/concert recording in berlin philharmonie

wilhelm furtwängler

brahms symphony no 3: fourth movement
unpublished radio recording with catalogue numbers
BLN 203.1505-1507

113/1932/hmv sessions in berlin singakademie
leo blech
cornelius der barbier von bagdad overture
2D 854   DB 4406
2D 855

cimarosa il matrimonio segreto overture
2D 856   DA 4404
2D 857

mozart die zauberflöte: marsch der priester
OD 893   DA 4405

schubert-webern deutsche tänze d820
2D 894   DB 4407
2D 895
lp: emi RLS 768/1C137 54095-54099

mozart kontretänze k535 and k609 no 1
2D 896   DB 1714

114/5 april 1932/telefunken session in berlin singakademie
leo blech
mendelssohn hebrides overture
18299   E 1090
18300
lp: melodiya M10 43567-43568

115/14 april 1932/telefunken session in berlin singakademie
hans schleger
mozart türkischer marsch; johann strauss persischer marsch
18325   A 1137
18326

adam si j'etais roi overture
18327   A 1095
18328

116/15 april 1932/telefunken session in berlin singakademie
selmar meyrowitz
liszt o lieb so lang du lieben kannst; ganne liebe himmlische macht; rubinstein melodie and elegie
with louis graveure, tenor
18329   unpublished
18330
18331   unpublished
18332

117/18 april 1932/concert recording in berlin philharmonie
wilhelm furtwängler
beethoven symphony no 9: unspecified extracts
with bruno-kittel-chor/ria ginster, soprano/frieda dieroff, contralto/
helge rosvaenge, tenor/rudolf bockelmann, bass-baritone
unpublished radio recording with catalogue numbers
BLN 204.1801-1804

118/28-30 may 1932/telefunken sessions in berlin
singakademie
hans schleger
kalman tanzen möcht' ich walzer; lehar evawalzer
18412   A 1126
18413

braga engellied; bose moorröschen
18414   A 1173
18420

zimmer japanischer laternentanz
18417   A 1170

119/31 may-2 june 1932/telefunken sessions in berlin singakademie

selmar meyrowitz

tchaikovsky symphony no 6: third movement
18421   F 1141
18422

tchaikovsky symphony no 5: second movement
18423   F 1191
18424

verdi i vespri siciliani overture
18425   E 1145
18426

tchaikovsky symphony no 6: fourth movement
18427   F 1218
18428

weber oberon: ozean du ungeheuer!
with gertrud bindernagel, soprano
18429   F 1144
18430
lp: telefunken 6.42332

verdi un ballo in maschera: eri tu; simon boccanegra: plebe! patrizi!
with hans reinmar, baritone/*sung in german*
18431   E 1160
18432
lp: preiser LV 83/telefunken H 17/GMA 57
cd: preiser 89112

120/6-8 june 1932/telefunken sessions in berlin singakademie
selmar meyrowitz/*paul kletzki
liszt o lieb so lang du lieben kannst; ganne liebe himmlische macht
with louis graveure, tenor
18440   A 1143
18441

wagner tristan und isolde: einsam wachend
with eva liebenberg, contralto
18444   unpublished

wagner lohengrin: in fernem land; rienzi: allmächtiger vater!
with louis graveure, tenor
18445   unpublished
18446

wagner tristan und isolde: mild und leise
with gertrud bindernagel, soprano
18458   F 1163
cd: teldec 8573 830222

*adagio from bach violin concerto in e bwv1042
with georg kulenkampff, violin
18451   F 1193/ultraphon F 22450
18452
lp: telefunken HT 6/6.48013/cd: pearl GEMMCD 9946

*beethoven romance in f op 50
with georg kulenkampff, violin
18453   F 1142/ultraphon F 22349
18454
lp: telefunken HT 6/6.48013/KT 11008/cd: pearl GEMMCD 9946

121/8-9 june 1932/telefunken sessions in berlin singakademie

selmar meyrowitz

wagner lohengrin: einsam in trüben tagen; tannhäuser: dich teure halle!
with hildegard ranczak, soprano
18457   unpublished
18459

puccini tosca: vissi d'arte: la boheme: si mi chiamano mimi
with hildegard ranczak/*sung in german*
18460   F 1197
18461

ponchielli la gioconda: dance of the hours
18462   E 1150/E 1710
18463

verdi aida: o patria mia!
with hildegard ranczak, soprano/*sung in german*
18464   F 1240
18465

122/16 june 1932/telefunken session in singakademie
hans schleger/*paul hörbiger
ketelby in a persian market
18472   A 1170

*dostal grosses wiener-lieder-potpourri
18473   E 1168
18474

ziehrer nachtschwärmerwalzer
18475   A 1169
18476

123/17 june 1932/telefunken session in singakademie
selmar meyrowitz
tchaikovsky ouverture solennelle "1812", abridged version
with chor der deutschen staatsoper
18477   E 1157
18478

offenbach orfee aux enfers overture
18479   E 1200
18480

124/18 june 1932/telefunken sessions in berlin singakademie
carl woitschach/*hans schleger
kermach rheinländer-potpourri
with frida weber-flessburg, soprano/alexander flessburg, tenor
18481   A 1171
18482

*bizet carmen-querschnitt
with anni frind, soprano/eva liebenberg, contralto/helge rosvaenge, tenor/wilhelm guttmann, baritone/*sung in german*
18485   E 1158
18486

125/23 june 1932/telefunken session in berlin singakademie
paul kletzki
mozart violin concerto no 5: third movement
with szymon goldberg, violin
18493   F 1234/SK 1234
18494
cd: symposium 1141/music and arts CD 1225

126/23-28 june 1932/telefunken sessions in berlin
singakademie

erich kleiber

heuberger der opernball overture
18489   E 1195/SK 1195
18490
cd: biddulph WHL 002/archiphon AEC 102/preiser 90395/
teldec 4509 955132

johann strauss wein weib und gesang waltz
18491   E 1206
18492
cd: preiser 90395/tahra TAH 358-361/teldec 4509 955132/
3984 284112

stravinsky feux d'artifice: reznicek donna diana overture
18495   E 1205
18496
cd: preiser 90311/archiphon ARC 102/telde 3984 284072

johann strauss 1001 nacht waltz
18497   E 1233
18498
lp: capitol P 8061
cd: preiser 90395/tahra TAH 358-361/teldec 3984 284112

johann strauss accelerationen waltz
18499   E 1156
18500
lp: capitol P 8061
cd: preiser 90395/tahra TAH 358-361/teldec 4509 955132/
3984 284072

126/june 1932/telefunken sessions in berlin/concluded

liszt venezia e napoli (tarantella), orchestral arrangement
18505   E 1154
18506
cd: berliner philharmoniker BPH 0603

beethoven symphony no 8: second movement;
deutscher tanz no 12
18507   E 1295
18508
lp: capitol P 8061 (deutscher tanz)

haydn 3 deutche tänze
18514   B 1340
18515

handel alcina: ballet music
18516   SK 1270
18517

127/27-30 june 1932/telefunken sessions in berlin
singakademie

erich orthmann

haydn deutschlandlied; gott mit uns
18501 unpublished
18502

friedrich der grosse fredericiana
18503 E 1153
18504

wagner tristan und isolde: einsam wachend
with eva liebenberg, contralto
18509 F 1163
lp: preiser LV 134
cd: preiser 89979

giordani caro mio ben; böhm still wie die nacht
with eva liebenberg, contralto
18520 A 1138
18521

128/3 august 1932/telefunken session in berlin singakademie

hans schleger

flotow alessandro stradella: jungfrau maria;
martha: ach so fromm
with constantin stellakis, tenor
18537   A 1159
18538

abt gute nacht; böhm hast du mich lieb?
with constantin stellakis, tenor
18539   A 1166
18540

brandt o maienzeit!; levi ich kam vom walde hernieder
with ulrich berner, baritone
18541   A 1167
18542

129/9-10 september 1932/telefunken sessions in berlin singakademie

hans schleger

preyer ob sie wohl kommen mag; lassen allerseelen
with ulrich berner, baritone
18608   A 1192
18609

potpourri of themes from d'albert's tiefland
18610   A 1194
18611

129/september 1932/telefunken sessions in berlin/concluded
schubert-berthe potpourri of themes from das dreimädlerhaus
with anni frind, soprano/liesl blech, soprano/luba schirmer, contralto/carl carli, tenor/ludwig van der sande, bass
18614   A 1198
18615

potpourri of themes from steffan's katharina
with chor der deutschen staatsoper/anni frind, soprano/constantin stellakis, tenor
18616   A 1199
18617

rosas über den wellen walzer
18619   A 1213

noak charakterstück aus heinzelmännchens wachparade
18624   A 1277

130/10 september 1932/odeon session in berlin
frieder weissmann
wagner rienzi overture
XXB 8550   O-6826/E 11218
XXB 8551

131/18-24 september 1932/telefunken sessions in berlin singakademie
selmar meyrowitz/*paul kletzki
puccini turandot: nessun dorma; non piangere liu
with constantin stellakis, tenor/*sung in german*
18612   A 1196
18613

puccini la fanciulla del west: ch'ella mi creda libero
with louis graveure, tenor/*sung in german*
18639   unpublished

*popper hungarian rhapsody in d
with emanuel feuermann, cello
18642   A 1235
18643

132/22-23 september 1932/telefunken sessions in berlin singakademie
hans schleger
translateur was blumen träumen walzer
18644   A 1213

potpourri on themes from hannemann's aus winkeln und gassen
18645   A 1274
18646

jones the geisha querschnitt
with sabine meyen, soprano/constantin stellakis, tenor/max kuttner,tenor
18648   A 1209
18649

133/17 october 1932/telefunken sessions in berlin singakademie
selmar meyrowitz
offenbach les contes d'hoffmann querschnitt
with hildegard ranczak, soprano/anni frind, soprano/ constantin stellakis. tenor/*sung in german*
18731 E 1238
18732

flotow martha: letzte rose
with hildegard ranczak, soprano
18733 unpublished

verdi il trovatore querschnitt
with hildegard ranczak, soprano/constantin stellakis, tenor/ *sung in german*
18734 unpublished
18735

thomas mignon: connais-tu le pays?
with anni frind, soprano/*sung in german*
18736 unpublished

134/17 october 1932/concert recording in berlin philharmonie
wilhelm furtwängler
reger variations and fugue on a theme of mozart: fugue
unpublished radio recording with catalogue numbers
BLN 210.1701-1703

135/25 october 1932/telefunken session in berlin singakademie
erich kleiber
meyerbeer das feldlager in schlesien overture
18741   F 1271/SK 1271
18742

weber preciosa overture
18743   E 1232
18744
cd: berliner philharmoniker BPH 0603

136/27 october 1932/concert recording in berlin philharmonie
wilhelm furtwängler
mozart sinfonia concertante k364: third movement
with szymon goldberg, violin/paul hindemith, viola
unpublished radio recording with catalogue numbers
BLN 210.2701-2702

137/1932/kristall session in berlin
julius prüwer
delibes coppelia ballet suite
2496   1047
2497
2498   1048
2499

138/december 1932/grammophon session in berlin hochschule für musik
wilhelm furtwängler
weber-berlioz aufforderung zum tanz
631   67056/brunswick 90313
632
lp: heliodor 88 021/deutsche grammophon 2535 821/ melodiya D 030275-030276
cd: dante LYS 116/koch 3-7073-2/naxos 8.111004/french furwängler society SWF 042-044/andromeda ANDRCD 5008

139/20 december 1932/concert recording in berlin philharmonie
wilhelm furtwängler
beethoven symphony no 8: second and third movements
unpublished radio recording with catalogue numbers
BLN 212.2001-2003

140/1933/deutsche wochenschau film footage in berlin philharmonie
max von schillings
rossini wilhelm tell overture
dvd: dreamlife (japan) DVLC 1009

141/1933/grammophon sessions in berlin lützowstrasse studio
max von schillings
schillings das hexenlied
with ludwig wüllner, speaker
678   67047/27429/35000
679
680   67048/27430/35001
681
682   67049/27431/35002
683
cd: preiser 90294

142/june-december 1933/grammophon sessions in berlin lützowstrasse studio
alois melichar
bach brandenburg concerto no 1 in f bwv1046
with szymon goldberg, violin/gustav kern, oboe
691   27313/decca LY 6082
692
740   27314/decca LY 6083
741
742   27315/decca LY 6084
cd: andante 1988/music and arts CD 1225

142/1933/grammophon sessions in berlin/concluded
bach brandenburg concerto no 4 in g bwv1049
with szymon goldberg, violin/albert harzer and heinrich breiden, flutes

699	27307/15238/decca LY 6069
700	
701	27308/15239/decca LY 6070
702	
703	27309/15240/decca LY 6071
704	

cd: music and arts CD 1225

bach brandenburg concerto no 6 in b flat bwv1051

749	15066/decca LY 6099
750	
751	15067/decca LY 6100
752	

143/1933/grammophon session in berlin lützowstrasse studio
paul graener
graener die flöte von sanssouci suite

710	15011
711	
712	15012
713	

144/1933/grammophon sessions in berlin lützowstrasse studio
alois melichar
fantasy on themes by tchaikovsky
        25188

saint-saens la princesse jaune overture
        25189/522687

blumen heiteres spiel für orchester
        25190

145/12-23 january 1933/telefunken sessions in berlin singakademie
hans unger
bach concerto in a minor bwv1065; vivaldi largo from a violin concerto
18863   SK 1317/TF 51
18864
18865   SK 1318/TF 52
18866

146/28 january 1933/telefunken session in singakademie
erich kleiber
suppe leichte kavallerie overture
18920   F 1322
18921
lp: capitol P 8108
cd: preiser 90395/berliner philharmoniker BPH 0603

147/6 february 1933/concert recording in philharmonie
wilhelm furtwängler
tchaikovsky symphony no 5: part of second movement
unpublished radio recording with catalogue numbers
BLN 302.0604-0606

148/28 february 1933/telefunken session in singakademie
franz alfred schmidt
massenet manon: ah fuyez douce image!;
meyerbeer l'africaine: o paradis!
with helge rosvaenge, tenor/*sung in german*
18978   SK 1407
18979
lp: preiser LV 515
cd: teldec 3984 284102 (manon)

149/7-8 march 1933/telefunken sessions in berlin singakademie
franz alfred schmidt/*gustav havemann
*wagner die meistersinger von nürnberg overture
18997   E 1349
18998

wagner götterdämmerung: starke scheite schichtet mir dort
with anny konetzni, soprano
18999   E 1362
19000
cd: preiser 89649/teldec 8573 830222

**wagner siegfried: nothung neidliches schwert!;
schmiede mein hammer!**
with willi störing, tenor
19001   E 1361/ultraphon G 22611
19002
cd: teldec 8573 830222

150/april 1933/telefunken session in berlin singakademie
franz alfred schmidt
gansser: deutschland erwache!; vitzthum das hakenkreuz
with gerhard hüsch, baritone
19038   A 1381
19039

151/27 may 1933/telefunken session in singakademie
wilhelm franz reuss
potpourri of themes by puccini
19122 E 1408
19123
19124 E 1409
19125

152/1 june 1933/telefunken session in singakademie
erich kleiber
tchaikovsky capriccio italien
19117 E 1406
19118

153/6-7 june 1933/telefunken sessions in singakademie
erich orthmann
potpourri of themes by verdi
19141 E 1455
19142
19143 E 1474
19144

puccini madama butterfly: addio fiorito asil; verdi la traviata: de miei bollenti spiriti
with helge rosvaenge, tenor/*sung in german*
19145 A 1538
19146
lp: preiser LV 515/telefunken HT 24
cd: pearl GEMMCD 9394/preiser 89201 (traviata)/89209 (butterfly)/ grammofono AB 78668-78669 (traviata)/teldec 3984 269192 (traviata)/3984 284102 (butterfly)

154/12-23 june 1933/telefunken sessions in berlin singakademie

eugen jochum

weber der freischütz overture
19159   E 1493
19160

wagner tannhäuser act three prelude
19161   unpublished

wagner tannhäuser overture; lohengrin act three prelude
19162   E 1424
19163
19164   E 1425
19200
cd: teldec 9031 764442 (tannhäuser)

wagner die meistersinger von nürnberg act three prelude
19198   A 1658
19199

155/19-23 june 1933/telefunken sessions in berlin singakademie
erich kleiber
johann strauss die fledermaus overture
19176 E 1536
19177
cd: biddulph WHL 002/preiser 90385/tahra TAH 358-361/teldec 4509 955132/3984 284072

johann strauss der zigeunerbaron overture
19178 E 1491
19179
cd: biddulph WHL 002/preiser 90229/90385/90900/tahra TAH 358-361/teldec 4509 955132/3984 284112

josef strauss dorfschwalben aus österreich waltz
19201 E 1422
19202

156/19 june 1933/telefunken session in berlin singakademie
erich orthmann
verdi otello: niun mi tema; aida: celeste aida
with helge rosvaenge, tenor/*sung in german*
19180 SK 1427
19181
lp: telefunken HT 24
cd: preiser 89209/teldec 3984 284102

157/20 june 1933/telefunken session in berlin singakademie
paul van kempen
bruch violin concerto no 1: second movement
with georg kulenkampff, violin
19182 E 1492
19183
lp: diskopedia MB 1015

brahms violin concerto: second movement
with georg kulenkampff, violin
19184 E 1423/TF 161/FP 1198/G 22455
19185
lp: diskopedia MB 1015

158/july 1933/grammophon sessions in berlin lützowstrasse studio
hans pfitzner
beethoven symphony no 8 in f op 93
704 15020/67276
705
706 15021/67277
707
708 15022/67278
709
lp: past masters PM 31/deutsche grammophon 2740 259
cd: preiser 90221/naxos 8.110910

159/17 august 1933/telefunken session in singakademie
wilhelm franz reuss
puccini la fanciulla del west: ch' ella mi creda libero; manon lescaut: donna non vidi mai
with peter anders, tenor/*sung in german*
19242   A 1478
19243
lp: telefunken HT 2/KT 11007

potpourri of themes from puccini's madama butterfly
19244   E 1588
19245

160/28 august 1933/telefunken session in singakademie
wilhelm franz reuss/*joseph müller
johann strauss die fledermaus querschnitt
with chor des deutschen opernhauses/erna berger, soprano/elisabeth friedrich, soprano/anni frind, soprano/charlotte müller, soprano/peter anders, tenor/eugen fuchs, baritone
19260   E 1456
19261
lp: capitol P 8034/telefunken HTP 156

*müller musik und liebe: mir hat ein märchen heut geträumt; nun ist frieden uns beschieden
with erna berger, soprano/peter anders, tenor
19262   A 1467
19263

161/1 september 1933/telefunken session in berlin singakademie
georg schumann
luther-schumann ein feste burg; mit fried und freud fahr ich dahin
with chor der berliner singakademie
19275   E 1442
19276

162/12 september 1933/telefunken sessions in berlin singakademie
wilhelm franz reuss
puccini tosca: e lucevan le stelle; recondita armonia
with marcel wittrisch, tenor/*sung in german*
19217   B 1434
19218

streifzug durch die johann-strauss-operetten
19302   unpublished
19303

163/25-27 september 1933/telefunken sessions in belin singakademie

wilhelm franz reuss

verdi otello: si per ciel marmoreo giuro
with marcel wittrisch, tenor/hans reinmar, baritone/*sung in german*
19314   E 1476
19315
lp: telefunken GMA 57
cd: preiser 89112

verdi aida querschnitt
with chor der städtischen oper/elsa wieber, soprano/margarete klose, contralto/willy störing, tenor/*sung in german*
19326   E 1475
19327

164/2 october 1933/telefunken session in singakademie

wilhelm franz reuss

strauss arabella: aber der richtige; du wirst mein gebieter sein
with marta fuchs, soprano/elsa wieber, soprano/paul schöffler, baritone
19330   E 1477
19331
lp: preiser LV 44

verdi otello: gia nella notte densa
with elsa wieber, soprano/marcel wittrisch, tenor/*sung in german*
19344   E 1504
19345

165/2-18 october 1933/telefunken sessions in berlin singakademie
hans bund
schenkendorf gott segne unsern führer; hermann mahnung
with marcel wittrisch, tenor
19348   A 1550
19349
cd: pool-musikproduktion 65023AV (schenkendorf)

liszt hungarian rhapsody no 2 in c minor
19367   E 1505
19368

166/23 october 1933/telefunken session in berlin singakademie
wilhelm franz reuss
humperdinck hänsel und gretel querschnitt
with chor der deutschen staatsoper/anni frind, soprano/ else rucziczka, soprano/eugen fuchs, baritone
19375   E 1508
19376

167/november 1933/grammophon sessions in berlin
hochschule für musik
wilhelm furtwängler
wagner götterdämmerung: siegfrieds trauermarsch
733   67054/91026/brunswick 90251/decca CA 8173
734
lp: heliodor 88 021/deutsche grammophon 2700 703/2721 113/
melodiya D 033213-033214
cd: symposium 1043/documents 20.3090/20.3092/223 508/koch
3-7073-2/deutsche grammophon 477 5238/naxos 8.111136/french
furtwängler society SWF 042-044/andromeda ANDRCD 5008

beethoven egmont overture
735   67055/brunswick 90250/decca CA 8170
736
45: deutsche grammophon EPL 30 540
lp: deutsche grammophon 2535 827/japan JP 110-112
cd: symposium 1043/grammofono AB 78574/dante LYS 074/
documents 20.3090/20.3093/223 508/deutsche grammophon
453 7002/453 8042/koch 3-7059-2/andromeda ANDRCD 5008/
french furtwängler society SWF 042-044/naxos 8.111003

**mozart le nozze di figaro overture; die entführung aus
dem serail overture**
737   35013/45130/brunswick 90402/decca CA 8187
738
45: deutsche grammophon EPL 30 172
lp: deutsche grammophon LPM 18 960/2535 827/
heliodor (usa) H 25079/HS 25079
cd: symposium 1043 (figaro)/dante LYS 117/deutsche grammophon
431 8732/documents 20.3090 (figaro)/20.3093 (figaro)/225 308
(figaro)/koch 3-7059-2/french furtwängler society SWF 042-044/
andromeda ANDRCD 5008/naxos 8.111136

168/13 november 1933/telefunken session in berlin singakademie
leo borchard
wagner die walküre: wotans abschied und feuerzauber
with hans reinmar, baritone

19431   E 1589
19432
19433   E 1590
19434

lp: telefunken HT 17
cd: teldec 8573 830222/testament SBT 1514

169/15 november 1933/concert recordings in berlin philharmonie at opening of reichskulturkammer
wilhelm furtwängler/*richard strauss
beethoven egmont overture
unpublished radio recording with catalogue numbers RRG 311.1501-1503

*strauss festliches präludium
unpublished radio recording with catalogue numbers RRG 311.1509-1511

170/20 november and 4 december 1933/telefunken sessions in singakademie
leo borchard
verdi don carlos: per me giunto
with hans reinmar, baritone/*sung in german*
19450   E 1494
19451
lp: preiser LV 83/telefunken GMA 57
cd: preiser 89112

puccini la boheme: che gelida manina; il trovatore: ah si ben mio
with marcel wittrisch. tenor/*sung in german*
19485   E 1495
19486

171/13 february 1934/telefunken sessions in singakademie
wilhelm franz reuss
johann-josef strauss pizzicato polka; helmesbeger ballsirenen; johann strauss 1001 nacht intermezo
19592   E 1622
19597

wagner die meistersinger von nürnberg: wach auf!; euch macht ihr's leicht; verachtet mir die meister nicht
with chor der städtischen oper/hans reinmar, baritone
19593   E 1610
19594
19595   E 1609
19596
lp: telefunken HT 17/GMA 57

172/14 february 1934/telefunken sessions in berlin singakademie
wilhelm franz reuss/*hans bund
*ippolitov-ivanov caucasian sketches
19598   E 1605
19599

zeller der vogelhändler querschnitt
with chor der städtischen oper/anita gura, soprano/anni frind, soprano/willy wörle, tenor
19600   E 1614
19601
cd: teldec 3984 284112

173/26 february 1934/telefunken session in berlin singakademie
wilhelm franz reuss
humperdinck königskinder: verdorben ach gestorben!;
marschner hans heiling: an jenem tag
with hans reinmar, baritone
19623   E 1657
19624
lp: telefunken GMA 57/preiser LV 83
cd: preiser 89112

174/5 march 1934/telefunken session in berlin singakademie
hans bund
kalman die zirkusprinzessin: zwei märchenaugen; lehar der zarewitsch: wolgalied
with marcel wittrisch, tenor
19631   E 1616
19632
lehar item also on E 2467

175/8 march 1934/telefunken sessions in berlin singakademie
rudolf schulz-dornburg
mozart piano concerto no 20 in d minor k466
with mitja nikisch, piano
19645   E 1643/ultraphon F 18037/F 22124
19646
19647   E 1644/ultraphon F 18038/F 22125
19648
19649   E 1645/ultraphon F 18039/F 22126
19650
19651   E 1646/ultraphon F 18040/F 22127
19652

176/27 march 1934/telefunken session in berlin singakademie
wilhelm franz reuss
verdi la forza del destino: solenne in quest' ora; puccini la boheme: o mimi tu piu non tormi
with marcel wittrisch, tenor/hans reinmar, baritone/*sung in german*
19706   E 1756
19707
lp: 6.42332 (puccini)/historia H 663-664 (verdi)

177/15-16 may 1934/telefunken sessions in singakademie
wilhelm franz reuss
verdi macbeth: patria oppressa!; otello: fuoco di gioa!
with chor der städtischen oper/*sung in german*
19847   E 1656
19848

rebikov berceuse
19849   A 1686/A 2552

178/23 may 1934/telefunken session in berlin singakademie
erich kleiber
mozart eine kleine nachtmusik k525
19852   E 1669/F 14424/capitol 89-80066
19853
19854   E 1670/F 14425/capitol 89-80067
19855
lp: capitol P 8038
cd: preiser 90229/doremi DHR 7752/musica classica 2003-2004/
berliner philhamoniker BPH 0603

179/8 june 1934/telefunken session in berlin singakademie
hans bund
länder und lieder: traditional songs from russia, germany,
france, italy, ireland, hungary, england, america
and austria
19859   E 1701
19860

180/11 june 1934/telefunken sessions in berlin singakademie
wilhelm franz reuss/*carl woitschach
*sousa marches: el capitan and stars and stripes forever
19871   A 1659
19872

potpourri of themes from puccini's tosca
19873   unpublished
19874

181/9 september 1934/telefunken sessions in berlin singakademie
paul hindemith
hindemith mathis der maler symphony
19762   E 1647/ultraphon F 14386/F 22349/decca GX 61001
19763
19764   E 1648/ultraphon F 14387/F 22350/decca GX 61002
19765
19766   E 1648/ultraphon F 14388/F 22351/decca GX 61003
19767
lp: capitol L 8003
cd: teldec 9031 764402/koch 311342

182/20 september 1934/telefunken session in berlin singakademie
erich kleiber
strauss der rosenkavalier: act three waltz sequence
20028   E 1688
20029
cd: biddulph WHL 002/teldec 3984 284072

nicolai die lustigen weiber von windsor overture
20030   E 1713/ultraphon F 22540
20031
cd: teldec 3984 284072

183/21 september-1 october 1934/telefunken sessions in berlin singakademie
leo borchard
suppe banditenstreiche overture
20032   A 1732
20033
lp: capitol P 8108
cd: testament SBT 1514

mendelssohn-andreae three piano fantasies
20034   A 1686
cd: testament SBT 1514

183/september-october 1934/telefunken sessions/concluded
potpourri of themes from puccini's tosca
20035   E 1714
20036

puccini madama butterfly: un bel di; tosca: non lo sospiri
with aulikki rautawaara, soprano/*sung in german*
20095   A 1689
20096

lp: telefunken HT 28

boccherini menuetto; haydn symphony no 88: fourth movement
20097   A 1711
20098
cd: testament SBT 1514

184/4-10 october 1934/telefunken sessions in berlin singakademie
hans schmidt-isserstedt
kalman die czardasfürstin querschnitt
with aulikki rautawaara, soprano/peter anders, tenor
20099   E 1690
20100

verdi il trovatore querschnitt
with chor der deutschen staatsoper/aulikki rautawaara, soprano/ margarete klose, contralto/peter anders, tenor/*sung in german*
20114   E 1715
20115

185/30 october 1934/telefunken session in singakademie
carl woitschach
fucik einzug der gladiatoren march; teike alte kameraden march
20207 A 1717
20208

186/31 october 1934/telefunken session in singakademie
carl schuricht
bach cantata no 50 "nun ist das heil und die kraft";
cantata no 104: du hire israel
with philharmonischer chor
20205 E 1709
20206
lp: capitol L 8077
cd: dante LYS 178

187/6-14 november 1934/telefunken sessions in berlin singakademie
leo borchard
grieg peer gynt suite no 1; solveig's song
20220 A 1726
20221
20222 A 1727
20223
cd: testament SBT 1514

187/6-14 november 1934/telefunken sessions/concluded
delibes coppelia: mazurka and valse
20245   A 1753
20246
cd: testament SBT 1514

delibes sylvia: intermezzo and pizzucato
20247   A 1729
20248
cd: testament SBT 1514 (pizzicato only)

188/21 november 1934/grammophon sessions in berlin lützowstrasse studios
alois melichar
bach brandenburg concerto no 5 bwv1050
with franz rupp, harpsichord
461   15073/decca LY 6101
462
463   15074/decca LY 6102
464
465   15075/decca LY 6103
466
467   15076/decca LY 6104

189/december 1934/telefunken sessions in singakademie
hans schmidt-isserstedt
rossini il barbiere di siviglia: una voce poco fa
with erna sack, soprano/*sung in german*
20316   E 1735
20317

donizetti don pasquale: son anchio' la virtu magica
with erna sack, soprano/*sung in german*
20335   E 1755
lp: capitol L 8119

190/20 december 1934/telefunken session in berlin singakademie
leo borchard
tchaikovsky casse noisette: danse chinois & danse des mirlitons
20373   A 1864
20374
cd: testament SBT 1514/tahra TAH 520

191/29 december 1934/telefunken session in berlin singakademie
carl schuricht
tchaikovsky suite no 3: theme and variations, abridged
20218   E 1752
20219
cd: dante LYS 180

tchaikovsky symphony no 4: second movement
20385   E 1791
20386
cd: dante LYS 180

192/1935-1937/deutsche wochenschau film footage in berlin philharmonie
eugen jochum
beethoven symphony no 5: opening bars
this material was originallu included in the film "botschafter der musik"

193/1935/grammophon sessions in berlin lützowstrasse studios/*hochschule für musik

alois melichar

*wagner tannhäuser: einzug der gäste

504	15457/57042

johann strauss die fledermaus overture

568	57029
569	

urbach am tchaikovsky-quell

653	57080
654	
655	57081
656	

strauss schlagobers: in der konditorei

732	27324/35011
633	

194/1935/grammophon sessions in berlin

peter raabe

beethoven piano concerto no 5 in e flat op 73 "emperor"

with wilhelm kempff, piano

570	67082/decca CA 8248
571	
572	67083/decca CA 8249
573	
574	67084/decca CA 8250
575	
576	67085/decca CA 8251
577	
578	67086/decca CA 8252

cd: deutsche grammophon 453 8042/music and arts CD 1071/ hänssler classics 94 045/appian APR 6019

195/january 1935/telefunken session in berlin

singakademie

friedrich jung

eine folge unserer schönsten lieder

with berliner liedtafel

20443	E 1741
20444	

196/4 january 1935/telefunken session in berlin singakademie
hans schmidt-isserstedt
verdi rigoletto: caro nome
with erna sack, soprano
20396   E 1755

popy suite orientale
20397   E 1760
20398

197/12-13 january 1935/telefunken sessions in berlin singakademie
kurt schröder/*hans schmidt-isserstedt
weber komponisten-porträt
with chor der berliner solistenvereinigung/elisabeth petzold, soprano/peter anders, tenor
20417   E 1792
20418

***rendezvous bei franz lehar**
with aulikki rautawaara, soprano/peter anders, tenor
20419   E 1781
20420
lp: telefunken HT 517

198/28 january 1935/telefunken sessions in berlin singakademie

erich kleiber

schubert symphony no 8 in b minor d759 "unfinished"

20458	E 1777
20459	
20460	E 1778
20462	
20462	E 1779
20463	

lp: telefunken MA 25008
cd: preiser 90229/teldec 9031 764362/
musica classica 2003-2004

199/12-18 february 1935/telefunken sessions in berlin singakademie

hans schmidt-isserstedt

grieg peer gynt: solveig's songs
with aulikki rautawaara, soprano

20549	E 1795
20550	

rimsky-korsakov sadko: chant hindou
with aulikki rautawaara, soprano

20551	unpublished

mascagni cavalleria rusticana: no no turiddu!
with aulikki rautawaara, soprano/peter anders, tenor

20570	E 1807

coupled with matrix number 20633 (session no. 200)

200/25 february-3 march 1935/telefunken sessions in berlin singakademie
hans schmidt-isserstedt
tartini concerto in d: grave ed espressivo
with gaspar cassado, cello
20607   E 1820

laserna tonadilla
with gaspar cassado, cello
20608   A 1830

rimsky-korsakov le coq d'or: hymne au soleil
with aulikki rautawaara, soprano
20632   unpublished

mascagni cavalleria rusticana: voi lo sapete
with aulikki rautawaara, soprano
20633   E 1807
coupled with 20570 (session no. 199)

haydn kaiser variations from string quartet op 76 no 2
20737   E 1828
20738

141

201/11 march 1935/telefunken sessions in singakademie
leo borchard/*hans schmidt-isserstedt
tchaikovsky sleeping beauty: waltz; casse noisette: overture, march, danse de la fee dragee, trepak and danse arabe
20657 A 1862
20658
20659 A 1863
20660
cd: testament SBT 1514/tahra TAH 520 (casse noisette)

*verdi la traviata acts one and three preludes
20661 E 1831
20662

202/14-15 march 1935/grammophon sessions in berlin lützowstrasse studios
alois melichar
schubert symphony no 8 in b minor d759 "unfinished"
5946   62721/10379/decca DE 7047
5947
5948   62722/10380/decca DE 7048
5949
5950   62723/10381/decca DE 7049
5951
5952   62724/10382/decca DE 7050
5953

203/16 march 1935/telefunken session in berlin singakademie
friedrich jung
eine folge unserer schönsten lieder (second series)
with berliner liedtafel
20671   E 1800
20672

204/21 march 1935/telefunken session in berlin singakademie
carl schuricht
bizet l'arlesienne suite no 1
20689   E 1850/E 285
20690
20691   E 1851/E 286
20692
lp: capitol L 8098
cd: iron needle IN 1393/dante LYS 180

205/27 march-1 april 1935/telefunken sessions in berlin singakademie
koichi kishi
kishi sketches of japan; japan suite
with maria basca, soprano
20698-20721 inclusive
only four of the twenty-four recorded sides were published:
disc numbers A 2003 and A 2004 (also on victor cd in japan)

206/3-4 april 1935/telefunken sessions in singakademie
hans schmidt-isserstedt
rossini wilhelm tell overture
20739   E 1803
20740

mendelssohn violin concerto in e minor op 64;
bach air from third orchestral suite
with georg kulenkampff, violin
20741   E 1824
20742
20743   E 1825
20744
20745   E 1826
20746
20747   E 1827
20748
lp: artisco C44G 0016-0017

207/8 april 1935/grammophon session in berlin
alois melichar
melichar baron-neuhaus-suite
5973   10367
5974
5975   10368
5976

208/15 april 1935/telefunken session in berlin singakademie
hans schmidt-isserstedt
spohr violin concerto no 8 "gesangsszene"; schumann abendlied
with georg kulenkampff, violin
20772   E 1847
20773
20774   E 1848
20775
20776   E 1849
20777
lp: discopedia BM 1015/melodiya M10 42819-42820
cd: alta nova NA 1

209/april 1935/telefunken session in berlin singakademie
hans schmidt-isserstedt
sibelius the first kiss; the tryst
with aulikki rautawaara, soprano
20810   A 1900
20811

210/may-june 1935/grammophon sessions in berlin hochschule für musik
wilhelm furtwängler
rossini il barbiere di siviglia overture
528   35028/91028/brunswick 95057/decca CA 8218
529
lp: heliodor 88 021/melodiya D 030275-030276
cd: symposium 1043/dante LYS 116/music and arts CD 954/koch 3-7059-2/french furtwängler society SWF 042-044/naxos 8.111003/ andromeda ANDRCD 5008/japanese furtwängler society WFJ 15-16

weber der freischütz overture and act three entr'acte
542   67108/566 177/brunswick 95030/decca CA 8262
543
544   67109/566 178/brunswick 95031/decca CA 8263
545
lp: rococo 2014/japan NA 121-122/deutsche grammophon 2535 821
cd: dante LYS 116/koch 3-7073-2/deutsche grammophon 459 0012 (overture)/459 0652 (overture)/documents 20.3090 (overture)/ 20.3093 (overture)/225 308 (overture)/naxos 8.111004/french furtwängler society SWF 042-044/andromeda ANDRCD 5008/ dutton CDVS 1920/japanese furtwängler society WFJ 22
entr'acte also published on 95411; WFJ 22 also claims to contain alternaive unpublished takes of the overture

211/17 may 1935/grammophon session in belin
lützowstrasse studios
alois melichar
ivanovici donauwellenwalzer
6045 10424
6036

johann strauss an der schönen blauen donau
6037 10598
6038

212/7 august 1935/telefunken experimental
langspielplatte sessions in berlin singakademie
hans schmidt-isserstedt
beethoven leonore no 3 overture
20878 unpublished

wagner der fliegende holländer overture
20879 unpublished

213/21 august 1935/telefunken sessions in singakademie
hans schmidt-isserstedt
lehar die lustige witwe querschnitt
chor der städtischen oper/anita gura, soprano/peter anders, tenor
20885   E 1866
20886
lp: capitol P 8139

d'albert tiefland querschnitt
with anita gura, sorano/carla spletter, mezzo-soprano/peter anders, tenor/hans hermann nissen, bass-baritone
20887   E 1873
20888

tchaikovsky komponisten-porträt
20889   E 1888
20890

214/6-9 september 1935/grammophon sessions in berlin lützowstrasse studios
alois melichar
setoguchi gunkan march; shikishimakan march
6144   47516/11273
6145
reissued on cd in japan

214/september 1935/grammophon sessions in berlin/concluded

suppe leichte kavallerie overture

6146   23934/10027/decca PO 5040
6147

boieldieu le caliphe de bagdad overture

6148   47107/23938/27164/decca PO 5073
6149

rossini wilhelm tell overture

6150   24155/10128/fonit 61051/decca PO 5074
6152
6153   24156/10129/fonit 61052/decca PO 5075

offenbach orfee aux enfers overture

6154   24233/decca PO 5085
6155

suppe, boieldieu and rossini items are incorrecly described by world's encyclopedia of recorded music as recordings by berlin staatskapelle

215/14 september 1935/telefunken sessions in berlin singakademie
hans schmidt-isserstedt
mozart le nozze di figaro overure
20924   A 2141

liszt komponisten-bildnis
with willy stech, piano
20925   E 1899
20926

sattler sternlein und mond; taubert der vogel im walde
with erna sack, soprano
20927   A 1868
20884

216/7 november 1935/telefunken sessions in berlin singakademie
artur rother
beethoven piano concerto no 3 in c minor op 37
with eduard erdmann, piano
20976   E 1889/ultraphon F 22546
20977
20978   E 1890/ultraphon F 22547
20979
20780   E 1891/ultraphon F 22548
20781
20782   E 1892/ultraphon F 22549
20783
cd: tahra TAH 199-200/classico PTC 2002

217/14 november 1935/telefunken sessions in berlin singakademie
hans schmidt-isserstedt
dvorak cello concerto in b minor op 104
with gaspar cassado, cello

20998	E 1893/ultraphon F 14392
20999	
21000	E 1894/ultraphon F 14393
21001	
21002	E 1895/ultraphon F 14394
21003	
21004	E 1896/ultraphon F 14395
21005	
21006	E 1897/ultraphon F 14396
21007	

218/1936/deutsche wochenschau film footage in berlin philharmonie
karl böhm/*leo borchard
johann strauss an der schönen blauen donau
part of this performance can be viewed in the fulm "botschafter der musik"

*johann strauss die fledermaus overture; die-fledermaus-potpourri; tritsch-tratsch polka
dvd: dreamlife (japan) DVLC 1009

219/28 february 1936/telefunken session in berlin
singakademie
hans schmidt-isserstedt
rossini il barbiere di siviglia overture
21147   E 1933
21148

strauss ständchen; wolf heimweh
with karl schmitt-walter, bass-baritone
21149   A 1946
21150

220/6 march 1936/electrola session in philharmonie
karl böhm
nicolai die lustigen weiber von windsor overture
2RA 1107   DB 4444
2RA 1108
lp: emi RLS 768/1C137 54095-54099
cd; warner classics 958 8672

wagner die meistersinger von nürnberg act three prelude
2RA 1109   EH 962
2RA 1110
lp: emi RLS 768/1C137 54095-54099
cd: warner classics 958 8672

221/8 april 1936/telefunken sessions in berlin singakademie
hans schmidt-isserstedt
thomas mignon querschnitt
with chor der deutschen staatsoper/ilse kögel, soprano/susi gmeiner, soprano/peter anders, tenor/hans hermann nissen, bass/*sung in german*
21215   E 2043
21216

weber der freischütz querschnitt
with ilse kögel, soprano/carla spletter, soprano/peter anders, tenor/hans hermann nissen, bass
21217   E 1943/ultraphon F 22568
21218

222/may 1936/telefunken session in berlin singakademie unnamed conductor
lincke frau luna: schlösser die im monde liegen;
im reich der indra: es war einmal
with karl schmitt-walter, bass-baritone
21249   A 2012
21250

223/25-28 june 1936/telefunken sessions in berlin singakademie
hans schmidt-isserstedt
schubert rosamunde: entr'acte no 2; ballet music no 2
21251   E 1902
21252

beethoven violin concerto in d op 61; mozart adagio in e minor k261
with georg kulenkampff, violin
21284   E 2016/G 70004/F 22550/TE 496
21285
21286   E 2017/G 70005/F 22551/TE 497
21287
21288   E 2018/G 70006/F 22552/TE 498
21289
21290   E 2019/G 70007/F 22553/TE 499
21291
21292   E 2020/G 70008/F 22554/TE 500
21293
21294   E 2021/G 70009/F 22555/TE 501
21295
lp: LE 6507/LGX 66017/HT 6/KT 11008/capitol P 8099

224/1 august 1936/film recording in olympia-stadion at opening ceremony of 1936 olympics
richard strauss
strauss olympische hymne
with bruno-kittel-chor
dvd: c major entertainment 729 908
footage originally seen in the film "triumph des willens"

225/19-21 october 1936/telefunken sessions in berlin singakademie
hans schmidt-isserstedt
bach italian concerto, orchestral arrangement; gluck ballet suite: gavotte and tambourin
21469   E 2079
21470
21471   E 2080
21476
lp: capitol L 8128 (bach)

226/23 december 1936/telefunken session in berlin singakademie
hans schmidt-isserstedt
liszt hungarian rhapsody no 1
21728   E 2146
21729

gounod faust: excerpts from the ballet music
21730   E 2150/ultraphon F 22358
21731

smetana furiant; lortzing holzschuhtanz
21732   A 2161
21733

mozart turkish march, orchestral arrangement
21740   A 2141

227/28 december 1936/grammophon sessions in berlin hochschule für musik

wilhelm furtwängler

mozart eine kleine nachtmusik k525

781	67156/67182/566 188/decca K 211
679	
680	67157/67183/566 189/decca K 212
681	
785	67158/67184/566 190/decca K 213

45: deutsche grammophon EPL 30 576
lp: deutsche grammophon LPM 18 960/2535 827/2730 005/
melodiya D 030275-030276/heliodor (usa) H 25079/HS 25079
cd: dante LYS 117/deutsche grammophon 431 8732/477 5238/
koch 3-7079-2/documents 20.3090/20.3091/223 508/
naxos 8.111136/french furtwängler soiety SWF 042=044/
andromeda ANDRCD 5008

679, 680 and 681 were recorded in june 1937

johann strauss die fledermaus overture

786	67121/91091/566 194
787	

lp: heliodor 88 021/melodiya D 030275-030276/japan AT 09-10
cd: preiser 90090/documents 20.3090/20.3093/223 508/
koch 3-7073-2/naxos 8.111005/andromeda ANDRCD 5008/
french furwängler society SWF 042-044

228/4 january 1937/columbia sessions in berlin
hidemaro konoye
mozart sinfonia concertante for wind k297b
with erich venske, oboe/alfred bürkner, clarinet/
oskar rothersteiner, bassoon/martin ziller, horn
CRX 46	LX 661/LFX 508
CRX 47	
CRX 48	LX 662/LFX 509
CRX 49	
CRX 50	LX 663/LFX 510
CRX 51	
CRX 52	LXS 664/LFX 511

78rpm edition also published in automatic coupling with the catalogue numbers LX 8346-8349

229/4 february 1937/telefunken session in berlin
singakademie
norbert schultze
marx marienlied; reger mariae wiegenlied
with erna sack, soprano
21789	A 2157
21790	

230/january-february 1937/telefunken session in berlin singakademie
leo borchard
francaix piano concertino
with jean francaix, piano
21816   E 2175/capitol 8-80108
21817
lp: capitol L 8051

231/march-april 1937/grammophon sessions in berlin hochschule für musik
alois melichar
sibelius finlandia
790   57068
791
according to michael gray further unidentified works were recorded at these sessions

232/13-14 april 1937/telefunken sessions in berlin singakademie
hans schmidt-isserstedt
lortzing zar und zimmermann overture
21995   A 2270
21996

verdi aida: grand march and ballet music
21997   E 2319/ultraphon F 22430
22004

232/april 1937/telefunken sessions in berlin/concluded

suppe die schöne galathea overture
21998   A 2318
21999

suppe pique dame overture
22000   A 2248
22001
lp: capitol P 8108

verdi la forza del destino overture
22002   E 2230
22003

tchaikovsky evgeny onegin: polonaise and waltz
22005   E 2231
22006

233/1 may 1937/hmv concert recording in london queens hall
wilhelm furtwängler
beethoven symphony no 9 in d minor op 125 "choral"
with philharmonic choir of london/erna berger, soprano/ gertrud pitzinger, contralto/walther ludwig, tenor/ rudolf watzke, bass

2EA 3559	unpublished
2EA 3560	
2EA 3561	unpublished
2EA 3562	
2EA 3563	unpublished
2EA 3564	
2EA 3565	unpublished
2EA 3566	
2EA 3567	unpublished
2EA 3568	
2EA 3569	unpublished
2EA 3570	
2EA 3571	unpublished
2EA 3572	
2EA 3573	unpublished
2EA 3574	
2EA 3575	unpublished
2EA 3576	
2EA 3577	unpublished

lp: emi ED 27 01231/toshiba WF 70073-70074
cd: toshiba TOCE 6067/dante LYS 073/music and arts CD 818/emi 562 8752/japanese furtwängler society WFJ 19/japanese furtwängler centre WFFC 0301

234/26 may 1937/telefunken sessions in singakademie
hans schmidt-isserstedt
lincke lysistrata: glühwürmchen-idyll. lehar gold und silber walzer
with chor der städtischen oper/erna sack, soprano
22083   E 2273
22084
cd: teldec 3984 284122

liszt hungarian rhapsody no 6
22085   E 2280
22086

gounod faust waltz; delibes naila waltz
22007   E 2247
22087

235/9 june 1937/telefunken sessions in singakademie
eugen jochum
beethoven symphony no 3 in e flat op 55 "eroica"
22144   E 2311/G 18001/G 22038/G 70101
22145
22146   E 2312/G 18002/G 22039/G 70102
22147
22148   E 2313/G 18003/G 22040/G 70103
22149
22150   E 2314/G 18004/G 22041/G 70104
22151
22152   E 2315/G 18005/G 22042/G 70105
22153
22154   E 2316/G 18006/G 22043/G 70106
cd: teldec 9031 764442

236/15 june 1937/telefunken session in singakademie
peter kreuder
johann strauss senior radetzky march
22164   A 2504

suppe flotte burschen overture
22165   A 2288
22166
lp: capitol P 8108

johann strauss eine nacht in venedig overture
22167   A 2258
22168

237/21 june 1937/telefunken sessions in singakademie
hans schmidt-isserstedt
brahms violin concerto in d op 77
with georg kulenkampff, violin
21389   E 2074/TE 528/ultraphon F 22556
21390
21391   E 2075/TE 529/ultraphon F 22557
21392
21393   E 2076/TE 530/ultraphon F 22558
21394
21395   E 2077/TE 531/ultraphon F 22559
21396
21397   E 2078/TE 532/ultraphon F 22560
lp: artisco C44 90016-90017
cd: pearl GEMMCD 9466

238/26 august 1937/telefunken sessions in singakademie
hans von benda
handel concerto in f for double wind; music for the royal fireworks: bourree, menuet and rejouissance
22238   E 2352
22239
22240   E 2353
22241

mozart symphony no 32 in g k318
22242   E 2317
22243
lp: capitol H 8131

239/30 august 1937/telefunken session in singakademie
eugen jochum
beethoven leonore no 3 overture
22244   E 2278
22245
22246   E 2279
22247

240/8 october and 3 november 1937/electrola sessions in berlin philharmonie

wilhelm furtwängler

beethoven symphony no 5 in c minor op 67

2RA 2335	DB 3328/victor M 426
2RA 2336	
2RA 2337	DB 3329/victor M 426
2RA 2338	
2RA 2339	DB 3330/victor M 426
2RA 2340	
2RA 2341	DB 3331/victor M 426
2RA 2342	
2RA 2343	DB 3332/victor M 426

lp: emi 2C051 03587/3C153 53800-53805M/french furtwängler society SWF 7002
cd: novello NVLCD 904/music and arts CD 954/dante LYS 072/ documents 20.3090/20.3095/223 508/biddulph WHL 006/ tahra FURT 1032-1033/naxos 8.110879/andromeda ANCRDC 5008/japanese furtwängler society WFJ 15-16

78rpm edition also published in automatic coupling with the catalogue numbers DB 8374-8378; japanese furtwängler society suggests that electrola and hmv used different takes of at least two of the 78rpm sides

241/8-15 november 1937 and 24 february-8 march 1938/
hmv sessions in berlin philharmonie

thomas beecham

mozart die zauberflöte

with berliner solistenvereinigung/tiana lemnitz, soprano/erna berger, soprano/irma beilke, soprano/helge rosvaenge, tenor/gerhard hüsch, baritone/wilhelm strienz, bass/walter grossmann, bass/hilde scheppan, soprano/elfriede marherr, soprano/carla spletter, soprano/ruth berglund, contralto/heinrich tessmer, tenor/ernst fabbry, tenor

2RA 2448	DB 3465/C 6371
2RA 2457	
2RA 2426	DB 3466/C 6372
2RA 2425	
2RA 2420	DB 3467/C 6373
2RA 2421	
2RA 2459	DB 3468/C 6374
2RA 2427	
2RA 2417	DB 3469/C 6375
2RA 2428	
2RA 2416	DB 3470/C 6376
2RA 2432	
2RA 2433	DB 3471/C 6377
2RA 2434	
2RA 2429	DB 3472/C 6378
2RA 2418	
2RA 2435	DB 3473/C 6379
2RA 2436	
2RA 2455	DB 3474/C 6380
2RA 2456	
2RA 2453	DB 3475/C 6381
2RA 2458	

241/november 1937-march 1938/hmv sessions in berlin/ concluded

2RA 2447	DB 3476/C 6382
2RA 2439	
2RA 2452	DB 3477/C 6383
2RA 2419	
2RA 2422	DB 3478/C 6384
2RA 2451	
2RA 2437	DB 3479/C 6385
2RA 2438	
2RA 2449	DB 3480/C 6386
2RA 2450	
2RA 2431	DB 3481/C 6387
2RA 2430	
2RA 2423	DB 3482/C 6388
2RA 2424	
	DB 3483/C 6389

45: victor WCT 56
lp: ALP 1273-1275/victor LCT 610/electrola E 80471-80473/
WCLP 616-618/world records SH 158-160/angel seraphim 6109/
turnabout THS 65078-65080/TV 4113=4115/
calig CAL 30845-30846/emi 143 4653
cd: emi 761 0342/nimbus NI 7827-7828/pearl GEMMCDS 9371/
melodram MEL 27056/naxos 8.110127-110128/dutton
CDEA 5011/arkadia 78027

the session on 8 march 1938 was used to re-record 2RA 2459 with erna berger and staatskapelle berlin conducted by bruno seidler-winkler; 78rpm edition was also published in automatic coupling with catalogue numbers DB 8475-8493; a two-part 78rpm edition was also published by victor with catalogue numbers M 541 and M 542

242/12-23 november 1937/grammophon sessions in berlin hochschule für musik

carl schuricht

beethoven symphony no 7 in a op 92

739	67162
740	
741	67163
742	
743	67164
744	
745	67165
746	
747	67166
748	

cd: dante LYS 177/shinseido (japan) SGR 6001-6005

243/19-20 november 1938/telefunken sessions in berlin singakademie

hans schmidt-isserstedt

suppe dichter und bauer overture
22596   A 2359
22597
lp: capitol P 8108

potpourri of themes by grieg
22598   E 2406
22599

suppe boccacio overture
22601   A 2403
22602
lp: capitol P 8108

massenet phaedra overture
22603   E 2399
22604

grieg letzter frühling
22607   E 2600

244/22 november 1937/odeon sessions in berlin odeon factory
hermann abendroth
beethoven symphony no 5 in c minor op 67

NSK 23	0-7898/parlophone E 11434
NSK 24	
NSK 25	0-7899/parlophone E 11435
NSK 26	
NSK 27	0-7900/parlophone E 11436
NSK 28	
NSK 29	0-7901/parlophone E 11437
NSK 30	

cd: tahra TAH 102/pristine audio PASC 256
tahra edition incorrectly dated 1939

244a/26 november 1937reichsrundfunk recording in berlin philharmonie
hans schmidt-isserstedt
schumann violin concerto in d minor
with georg kulenkampff, violin
unpublished recording of the world premiere performance

245/20 december 1937/telefunken sessions in berlin
singakademie
hans schmidt-isserstedt
schumann violin concerto in d minor
with georg kulenkampff, violin
22686   E 2395/TE 655
22687
22688   E 2396/TE 656
22689
22690   E 2397/TE 657
22691
22692   E 2398/TE 658
lp: telefunken HT 5/6.48013/melodiya M10 42819-42820
cd: teldec 8.43765/4509 936722/dutton CDBP 5018

246/22 december 1937/grammophon session in berlin hochschule für musik
paul van kempen
liszt les preludes
751   67174
752
753   67175
754

247/10 january 1938/telefunken sessions in berlin singakademie
hans von benda
schubert symphony no 5 in b flat d485
22738   E 2516
22739
22740   E 2517
22741
22742   E 2518
22743

248/11 february 1938/electrola session in philharmonie
wilhelm furtwängler
wagner tristan prelude and liebestod
2RA 2657   DB 3419/victor M 653
2RA 2658
2RA 2659   DB 3420/victor M 653
2RA 2660
lp: SME 91399/hmv COLH 307/unicorn WFS 2-3/melodiya D 03367-8/
angel seraphim 6024/top classic TC 9054/emi 2C061 00932/
1C149 01197-01199M/F666 701/bayreuth festival 1976
cd: dante LYS 115/music and arts CD 954/biddulph WHL 006/
documents 222 128/emi 764 9352/andromeda ANDRCD 5008/
naxos 8.110865

249/14 february 1938/telefunken session in singakademie
eduard künnecke
künnecke tänzerische suite; glückliche reise overture
22853   E 2490
22854
22855   A 2491
22856
22857   E 2492
22858
22859   A 2493
22860
22861   E 2494
22862

250/19-21 february 1938/telefunken sessions in berlin singakademie
igor stravinsky
stravinsky jeu de cartes
22884   SK 2460
22885
22886   SK 2461
22887
22888   SK 2462
22889
lp: capitol L 8028/mercury MG 10014
cd: teldec 9031 764402

251/24 february 1938/electrola session in berlin philharmonie
bruno seidler-winkler
mozart le nozze di figaro: porgi amor; dove sono
with tiana lemnitz, soprano
2RA 2697   DB 3462
2RA 2698
45: E 40074/7EW 118381
lp: victor LCT 6701/rococo 5273 (dove sono)/preiser LV 101/
arabesque 8028/world records SHB 47/emi 1C147 28989-28990/
EX 29 05983/historia H 704-705 (dove sono)
cd: preiser 80902/89025/emi 763 7502/zyx music PD 50182

252/25 february 1938/telefunken session in singakademie
rolf schröder
johann strauss kaiserwalzer, vocal version
with erna sack, soprano
22906   E 2495
22907
cd: teldec 3984 284122

253/26 february-1 march 1938/grammophon sessions in berlin hochschule für musik
carl schuricht
bruckner symphony no 7 in e
912	67195
913	
914	67196
915	
916	67197
790	
917	67198
918	
919	67199
920	
921	67200
922	
923	67201
924	
925	67202

cd: shinseido (japan) SGR 6006-6007

254/5-8 march 1938/grammophon sessions in berlin hochschule für musik

walter davisson

beethoven violin concerto in d op 61

with karl freund, violin

580	15205
581	
802	15206
803	
804	15207
805	
643	15208
807	
808	15209
809	

255/10-11 march 1938/telefunken sessions in berlin singakademie

hans schmidt-isserstedt

sibelius valse triste

22605   E 2908

grieg herzwunden

22606   E 2600

verdi aida: prelude and ballet music

22940   E 2601
22945

255/10-11 march 1938/telefunken sessions/concluded
chabrier espana
22943   E 2624
22944

mozart cosi fan tutte overture; die entführung aus dem serail overture
22946   E 2522
22947
entführung overture also issued on ultraphon F 22240

mozart die zauberflöte overture
22948   E 2627
22949

256/14-18 march 1938/grammophon sessions in berlin hochschule für musik
alois melichar
josef strauss dorfschwalben aus österreich
823   15204
824

josef strauss sphärenklänge
828   15200
829

johann strauss g'schichten aus dem wienerwald; 1001 nacht walzer
859   15215
860
861   15216
862

257/15 march 1938/electrola session in berlin philharmonie
wilhelm furtwängler
wagner parsifal prelude and karfreitagszauber
2RA 2741   DB 3445/victor M 514
2RA 2742
2RA 2743   DB 3446/victor M 514
2RA 2744
2RA 2745   DB 3447/victor M 514
2RA 2746
lp: SME 91399/SMVP 8055-8056/hmv COLH 307/unicorn WFS 2-3/
angel seraphim 6024/top classic TC 9054/emi 29 12343/
RLS 768 (karfreitagszauber)/1C147 29229-29230/
1C149 01197-01199M/acanta 40 23520 (prelude)/
discocorp RR 229 (prelude)
cd: acanta 43 121 (prelude)/44 1055 (prelude)/documents
20.3090/20.3092/223 508/magic talent MT 48090 (prelude)/
grammofono AB 78515 (prelude)/dante LYS 115/iron needle
IN 1364-1365 (prelude)/biddulph WHL 006/emi 764 9352/
naxos 8.110879/andromeda ANDRCD 5008/archipel ARPCD 0261
78rpm edition was also published in automatic coupling with catalogue numbers DB 8494-8495

258/12 april 1938/telefunken sessions in berlin singakademie
hans schmidt-isserstedt
jaernefelt berceuse
23019   E 2545

beethoven adagios from piano sonatas nos 8 and 13, orchestral arrangements
23020   A 2544
23021

258/12 april 1938/telefunken sessions in berlin/concluded
kilpinen folksong from kukon kuullessa
with aulikki rautawaara, soprano
23022   A 2542
23023
lp: capitol L 8041

sibelius schilflied; diamond in the snow
with aulikki rautawaara, soprano
25024   A 2519
25025
lp: capitol L 8041

259/14 april 1938/grammophon session in hochschule für musik
leopold ludwig
handel movements from organ concerti
with alfred sittard, organ
901   67258
902
903   67259
904

260/21 april 1938/grammophon sessions in lützowstrasse studios
hidemaro konoye
national anthems of japan and germany; horst-wessel-lied
7741   11273/2910 (japan)
7742

haydn symphony no 91 in e flat
7743   62792/561135/fonit 81036/decca PO 5130
7744
7745   62793/561136/fonit 81037/decca PO 5131
7746
7747   62794/561137/fonit 81038/decca PO 5132
7748

mussorgsky night on bare mountain
854   67259/fonit 91129
855
issued on cd in japan

261/22 april and 15 june 1938/telefunken sessions in singakademie

hans von benda

respighi ancient airs and dances third suite; corelli gigue and badinerie from suite for strings

23059   E 2535/capitol ECL 8056
23060
23061   E 2536/capitol ECL 8056
23062
23063   E 2537/capitol ECL 8056
23064
lp: capitol P 8059

dvorak serenade for strings

23239   E 2650/capitol ECL 8055
23240
23241   E 2651/capitol ECL 8055
23242
23243   E 2652/capitol ECL 8055
23244
lp: capitol P 8004/P 8060

262/29-30 august and 20 september 1938/telefunken sessions in berlin singakademie

eugen jochum

brahms symphony no 1 in c minor op 68

23362   E 2703
23363
23364   E 2704
23365
23366   E 2705
23367
23368   E 2706
23369
23370   E 2707
23371

wagner tristan prelude and liebestod

23372   E 2715
23373
23374   E 2716
23375

beethoven egmont overture

23376   E 2683
23377

262/august-september 1938/telefunken sessions/concluded
beethoven symphony no 7 in a op 92
23466	SK 2763/ultraphon G 18007
23467	
23468	SK 2764/ultraphon G 18008
23469	
23470	SK 2765/ultraphon G 18009
23471	
23472	SK 2766/ultraphon G 18010
23473	
23474	SK 2767/ultraphon G 18011
23475	

263/9 september 1938/electrola sessions in philharmonie
hans weisbach
tchaikovsky serenade for strings: third and fourth movements
2RA 3212	DB 4586
2RA 3213	

liszt hungarian fantasy for piano and orchestra
with winifried wolf, piano
2RA 3214	EH 1209/JH 225
2RA 3215	
2RA 3216	EH 1210/JH 226
2RA 3217	

264/14-15 september 1938/telefunken sessions in berlin singakademie

hans schmidt-isserstedt

wagner götterdämmerung: siegfrieds rheinfahrt
23443   E 2685
23444

wagner das rheingold: einzug der götter in walhall
23445   E 2783
23446

wagner die meistersinger von nürnberg: tanz der lehrbuben; die walküre: walkürenritt
23447   E 2746
23448

auber la muette de portici overture
23449   E 2686
23450

rossini l'italiana in algeri overture
23451   E 2745
23452

rossini la scala di seta overture
23453   E 2717
23454

265/15 september 1938/telefunken session in berlin singakademie
walter lutze
strauss heimliche aufforderung; ständchen
with peter anders, tenor
23455   A 2684
23456
45: UV 244
lp: HT 36/648.064/628.636

strauss ich trage meine minne; traum durch die dämmerung
with peter anders, tenor
23457   A 2782
23458
45:   UV 244
lp: HT 36/648.064/628.636

266/1 october 1938/odeon sessions in philharmonie
hermann abendroth
beethoven fidelio overture
BE 12177   0-4617/0-188100
BE 12178

liszt hungarian rhapsody no 2
XXB 8675   0-7887/parlophone E 11389
XXB 8676
cd: pristine audio PASC 256

wagner der fliegende holländer overture
XXB 8677   0-7888/parlophone E 11422
XXB 8678
lp: emi RLS 768/1C137 54095-54099
cd: emi CDF 300 0122

267/25-27 october 1938/electrola sessions in philharmonie
wilhelm furtwängler
tchaikovsky symphony no 6 in b minor op 74 "pathetique"

2RA 3345	DB 4609/victor M 553
2RA 3346	
2RA 3347	DB 4610/victor M 553
2RA 3348	
2RA 3349	DB 4611/victor M 553
2RA 3353	
2RA 3354	DB 4612/victor M 553
2RA 3355	
2RA 3356	DB 4613/victor M 553
2RA 3350	
2RA 3351	DB 4614/victor M 553
2RA 3352	

lp: E 91079/hmv COLH 21/TRX 6140/world records H 107/
emi RLS 768/ F669.711-715/melodiya D 020049-020050/
cd: novello NVLCD 904/claremont GSE 78 5051/palladio PD 4122/
historical performers HP 14/grammofono AB 78558/documents
20.3090/20.3091/223 508/music and arts CD 954/emi 764 8552/
300 0122/907 8782/biddulph WHL 007/naxos 8.110865/
andromeda ANDRCD 5008/dutton CDVS 1920/tahra
FURT 1099-1100/japanese furtwängler society WFJS 15-16
78rpm edition was also published in automatic coupling
with catalogue numbers DB 8600-8605

268/20 december 1938/telefunken session in berlin singakademie
hans von benda
boccherini cello concerto in b flat
with tibor de machula, cello

23757	E 2778
23758	
23759	E 2779
23760	

269/9-14 january 1939/telefunken sessions in berlin singakademie
hans schmidt-isserstedt
tchaikovsky piano concerto no 1 in b flat minor op 23
with konstantin konstantinoff, piano

23791	E 2810
23792	
23793	E 2811
23794	
23795	E 2812
23796	
23797	E 2813
23798	

liszt piano concerto no 2 in a
with konstantin konstantinoff, piano

23825	unpublished
23826	
23827	unpublished
23828	

270/1939/deutsche wochenschau film footage in berlin philharmonie
eugen jochum
wagner die walküre: wotans abschied und feuerzauber
with hans reinmar, baritone
this footage was included in the film "musikstadt berlin"

271/19 january 1939/reichsrundfunk recording without audience in berlin philharmonie
wilhelm furtwängler
furtwängler symphonic concerto in b minor
with edwin fischer, piano
EA 50570   unpublished
EA 50571
EA 50572   unpublished
EA 50573
EA 50574   unpublished
EA 50575
EA 50576   unpublished
EA 50577
EA 50578   unpublished
EA 50579
EA 50580   unpublished
EA 50581
EA 50582   unpublished
EA 50583
EA 50584   unpublished
EA 50585
EA 50586   unpublished
EA 50587
cd: pilz CD 78004/dante LYS 123

272/8-9 february 1939/telefunken sessions in singakademie
hans schmidt-isserstedt
smetana ma vlast: the moldau; dvorak slavonic dance op 46 no 2
23896   E 2828
23897
23898   E 2829
23896

schmidt notre dame intermezzo
23899   E 2908

haydn symphony no 94 in g "surprise"
23900   E 2864/capitol ECL 8021
23901
23902   E 2865/capitol ECL 8021
23903
23904   E 2866/capitol ECL 8021
23905
lp: capitol P 8038

273/21 february 1939/grammophon session in berlin alte-jakob-strasse
alois melichar
melichar wiener impressionen
8302   11123
8303
8304   11124
8305

bach-melichar toccata and fugue bwv565
1044   15243
1045

274/7 march 1939/electrola sessions in berlin philharmonie
johannes schüler
beethoven violin romances nos 1 and 2
with siegfried borries, violin
2RA 3780   DB 4661
2RA 3781
2RA 3782   DB 4662
2RA 3783

blacher concertante musik
2RA 3784   DB 4618
2RA 3785

275/11 march-12 april 1939/grammophon sessions in berlin alte-jakob-strasse studio
victor de sabata
brahms symphony no 4 in e minor op 98
1057   67490/cetra OR 5001/decca LY 6171
1059
1060   67491/cetra OR 5002/decca LY 6172
1061
1062   67492/cetra OR 5003/decca LY 6173
1064
1068   67493/cetra OR 5004/decca LY 6174
1069
1070   67494/cetra OR 5005/decca LY 6175
1079
1080   67495/cetra OR 5006/decca LY 6176
lp: decca (usa) DL 9516/heliodor 88 001/
deutsche grammophon 2535 812/2548 703
cd: 423 7152/479 8196/pearl GEMS 0054/istituto discografico italiano IDIS 6406-8407

275/march-april 1939/grammophon sessions/continued
strauss tod und verklärung
1072   67516
1074
1076   67517
1097
1107   67518
1108
lp: heliodor 88 002
cd: 423 7152/479 8196/pearl GEMS 0054/istituto discografico italiano IDIS 6406-6407

respighi feste romane
1087   67510
1088
1089   67511
1090
1094   67512
1095
1096   67513
lp: discocorp IGI 356
cd: 479 8196/koch 3-7126-2/pearl GEMS 0054/istituto discografico italiano IDIS 6406-6407

wagner tristan prelude and liebestod
1092   67496
1098
1099   67497
1105
1106   67498
lp: heliodor 88 002
cd: 479 8196/koch 3-7126-2/pearl GEMS 0054/istituto discografico italiano IDIS 6406-6407

275/march-april 1939/grammophon sessions/concluded
kodaly dances of galanta
1100   67525
1101
1102   67526
1103
lp: decca (usa) DL 9513/deutsche grammophon LPEM 19 078/
2548 703/heliodor 88 001
cd: 479 8196/koch 3-7156-2/pearl GEMS 0054/istituto
discografico italiano IDIS 6406-6407

verdi aida prelude
1104   68395
lp: heliodor 88 002
cd: 479 8196/koch 3-7126-2/istituto discografico italiano IDIS 6406-6407

276/25 april 1939/electrola session in berlin philharmonie
wilhelm furtwängler
furtwängler symphonic concerto: second movement
with edwin fischer, piano
2RA 3904   DB 4696
2RA 3905
2RA 3906   DB 4697
lp: french furtwängler society SWF 7101/japan 1101-1102/
emi HLM 7027/1C047 01415M/discocorp MLG 74
cd: music and arts CD 954/documents 20.3090/20.3093/
223 508/biddulph WHL 007/testament SBT 1170/naxos
8.110879/andromeda ANDRCD 5008/emi 907 878

277/1-5 june 1939/grammophon sessions in berlin
alte-jakob-strasse studios
max fiedler
brahms piano concerto no 2 in b flat op 83
with elly ney, piano
1139	67566/G 19027
1141	
1142	67567/G 19028
1143	
1144	67568/G 19029
1145	
1146	67569/G 19030
1147	
1470	67570/G 19031
1471	
1472	67571/G 19032
1473	

lp: decca (usa) DL 9563/heliodor 88 010
cd: biddulph WHL 003-004/pristine audio PASC 363
parts of this recording were remade in april 1942 with an unnamed conductor

278/23 june 1939/grammophon sessions in berlin alte-jakob-strasse studios

herbert von karajan

tchaikovsky symphony no 6 in b minor op 74 "pathetique"

1189	67499
1190	
1191	67500
1192	
1193	67501
1194	
1195	67502
1196	
1197	67503
1198	
1199	67504
1200	

lp: top classic TC 9055
cd: deutsche grammophon 423 5302/423 5252/477 6237/ unlimited classics HDNC 0017
some issues were incorrectly dated april 1939

279/13 september 1939/reichsrundfunk recordings without audience in berlin philharmonie

wilhelm furtwängler

handel concerto grosso in d op 6 no 5

EA 55966	unpublished
EA 55967	
EA 55968	unpublished
EA 55969	
EA 55970	unpublished

cd: tahra FURT 1014-1015/documents 20.3090/20.3093/223 508

beethoven symphony no 5 in c minor op 67

EA 55971	unpublished
EA 55972	
EA 55973	unpublished
EA 55974	
EA 55975	unpublished
EA 55976	
EA 55977	unpublished
EA 55978	
EA 55979	unpublished
EA 55980	

cd: tahra FURT 1014-1015

matrix EA 55979 being missing from the source, it is replaced by tahra with the same section from the 1937 electrola recording (session no. 240)

280/14 november 1939/deutsche wochenschau film footage in berlin philharmonie
george georgescu
strauss till eulenspiegels lustige streiche
this footage can be viewed in the films "botschafter der musik" and "musikstadt berlin"

281/6-7 december 1939/telefunken sessions in berlin singakademie
hans schmidt-isserstedt
bizet l'arlesienne suite no 2
24717   E 3061/TE 899
24718
24719   E 3062/TE 900
24720
lp: capitol L 8078

mozart don giovanni overture
24721   E 3072/ultraphon F 22238
24722

dvorak carnival overture
24723   E 3053/ultraphon F 22426
24724

liadov the enchanted lake
24725   E 3059/ultraphon F 18050
24726

282/30 march 1940/reichsrundfunk recording in berlin
artur rother
weber oberon overture
lp: avon AV 3014

283/1 april 1940/grammophon sessions in berlin
alte-jakob-strasse studios
walter gmeindl
haydn symphony no 92 in g "oxford"
1454   67456/67562/fonit 96089
1455
1456   67457/67563/fonit 96090
1457
1458   67458/67564/fonit 96091
1459
1460   67459/67565/fonit 96092
1461

284/30 april 1940/grammophon sssion in berlin
alte-jakob-strasse studios
alois melichar
lortzing der waffenschmied overture
1475   15320
1476

285/6-22 june 1940/grammophon sessions in alte-jakob-strasse
herbert von karajan
smetana ma vlast: the moldau

1482	67583
883	
884	67584
885	

lp: deutsche grammophon LPEM 19 078
cd: deutsche grammophon 423 5302/423 5252/477 6237/ unlimited classics HDNC 0017
matrix 1482 was recorded on 9 june 1941

johann strauss künstlerleben waltz

886	67585
887	

cd: deutsche grammophon 423 5302/423 5252/477 6237/ unlimited classics HDNC 0017/pristine audio PACO 070

dvorak symphony no 9 in e minor op 95 "from the new world"

890	67519/cetra OR 5019
891	
892	67520/cetra OR 5020
893	
894	67521/cetra OR 5021
895	
900	67522/cetra OR 5022
901	
902	67523/cetra OR 5023
903	
904	67524/cetra OR 5024
905	

cd: deutsche grammophon 423 5282/423 5252/477 6237/ unlimited classics HDNC 0017
johann strauss and dvorak items were incorrectly dated february-march 1940

286/8-11 july 1940/telefunken magnetophon sessions in berlin philarmonie

willem mengelberg

tchaikovsky symphony no 5 in e minor op 64

25071	SK 3086/capitol EFL 8053
25072	
25073	SK 3087/capitol EFL 8053
25074	
25075	SK 3088/capitol EFL 8053
25076	
25077	SK 3089/capitol EFL 8053
25078	
25079	SK 3090/capitol EFL 8053
25080	
25081	SK 3091/capitol EFL 8053
25082	

45: capitol KFM 8053/EFM 8090
lp: HT 4/GM 69/KT 11010/648.014/capitol P 8053
cd: teldec 844.161/243.7272/biddulph WHL 051/dante LYS 189/ warner (japan) WQCC 351-354/pristine audio PASC 348

tchaikovsky piano concerto no 1 in b flat minor op 23
with conrad hansen, piano

25083	SK 3092/T 76/ultraphon G 14273
25084	
25085	SK 3093/T 77/ultraphon G 14274
25086	
25087	SK 3094/T 78/ultraphon G 14275
25088	
25089	SK 3095/T 79/ultraphon G 14276
25090	

lp: capitol P 8097/past masters PM 18
cd: teldec 844.160/243.7262/biddulph WHL 051/dante LYS 239/ warner (japan) WQCC 351-354/pristine audio PASC 348

287/3-4 september 1940/grammophon sessions in berlin alte-jakob-strasse studios

georg hoeberg/*emil reesen
*lange-müller renaissance: overture from the incidental music;
gade a folk tale: polonaise and bridal waltz
948   15358/polyphon (denmark) ZS 60103
951
cd: classico CLASSCD 513

lange-müller once upon a time: table music: nocturne;
wedding music; midsummer song
949   15357/polyphon (denmark) ZS 60102
950
cd: classico CLASSCD 513

*lumbye dream pictures
952   15355/polyphon (denmark) ZS 60100
953
cd: classico CLASSCD 513

kuhlau elves' hill overture
954   15356/polyphon (denmark) ZS 60101
955
cd: classico CLASSCD 513

*nielsen maskerade: overture and dance of the cockerels
956   15354/polyphon (denmark) ZS 60099
957
cd: classico CLASSCD 513

288/3-4 september 1940/grammophon sessions in berlin
alte-jakob-strasse studios
heinz schubert
heinz schubert prelude and toccata
with erich röhn, violin/reinhart wolf, viola/tibor de machula, cello
1064   67601
1065
1066   67602
1067

heinz schubert concertante suite
              57358

289/21 september 1940/grammophon sessions in berlin
alte-jakob-strasse studios
hans pfitzner
pfitzner symphony no 2 in c op 46
1519   67604
1520
1521   67605
1522
1523   67606
lp: heliodor 88 014
cd: preiser 90029

290/15 october 1940/telefunken magnetophon session in berlin philharmonie
wilhelm furtwängler
beethoven grosse fuge from quartet op 130, orchestral arrangement
23238   SK 3104
25239
45: LV 115
lp: LS 6025/capitol H 8130/rococo 2013/japan JP 1101-1102/AT 07-08/ french furtwängler society SWF 7702
cd: french furtwängler society SWF 901/teldec 9031 764352/ music and arts CD 954/tahra FURT 1012-1013/naxos 8.110095/ andromeda ANDRCD 5008

291/23 november 1940/grammophon session in berlin alte-jakob-strasse studios
franco ferrara
verdi vespri siciliani overture
unpublished

292/18 december 1940/telefunken sessions in berlin singakademie
hans schmidt-isserstedt
haydn cello concerto in d
with gaspar cassado, cello
25450   SK 3222
25451
25452   SK 3223
25453
25454   SK 3224
25455

293/4 january 1941/reichsrundfunk recordings without audience in berlin haus des rundfunks
hans knappertsbusch
liszt les preludes; nicolai die lustigen weiber von windsor overture
EA 63007   unpublished
EA 63008
EA 63009   unpublished
EA 63010
EA 63011   unpublished
EA 63012
EA 63013   unpublished
EA 63014
cd: tahra TAH 309/archiphon ARC 110-111

294/2-4 february 1941/acetates from reichsrundfunk recording in berlin philharmonie
wilhelm furtwängler
bruckner symphony no 7 in e
lp: japan AT 11-12
the recordng has many gaps in the music, with the final movement missing entirely

295/7 march 1941/odeon session in berlin
fritz lehmann
boccherini menuetto; haydn serenade from quartet op 3 no 5
BE 12837   O-4634
BE 12838

mozart eine kleine nachtmusik k525
XXB 8758   O-7942
XXB 8759
XXB 8760   O-7943
XXB 8761
lp: emi RLS 768/1C137 54095-54099
cd: emi CDF 300 012

296/17 march-9 april 1941/grammophon sessions in berlin alte-jakob-strasse studios
leopold ludwig
mozart symphony no 39 in e flat k543
1296   67613/fonit 91138
1297
1298   67614/fonit 91139
1299
1300   67615/fonit 91140
1301

296/march-april 1941/grammophon sessions/concluded
haydn symphony no 103 in e flat "drumroll"

1604	67616
1605	
1606	67617
1607	
1612	67618
1613	
1614	67619
1615	

297/7 april 1941/grammophon sessions in berlin alte-jakob-strasse
paul van kempen
beethoven symphony no 8 in f op 93

1333	67662/G 19024/cetra OR 5083
1334	
1335	67663/G 19025/cetra OR 5084
1640	
1641	67664/G 19026/cetra OR 5085
1642	

cd: tahra TAH 512-515

recording was completed on 4 october 1941

298/9 june 1941/grammophon session in berlin
alte-jakob-strasse studios
herbert von karajan
johann strauss kaiserwalzer
1483   67649
1484
cd: deutsche grammophon 423 5282/423 5252/477 6237/unlimited classics HDNC 0017/pristine audio PACO 070

299/12 june 1941/imperial sessions in berlin
johannes schüler
schubert symphony no 8 in b minor d759 "unfinished"
KC 0306   014042
KC 0307
KC 0308   014043
KC 0309
KC 0310   014044
KC 0311

300/16 june and 2 july 1941/odeon sessions in berlin
arthur grüber
borodin prince igor: polovtsian dances and march
XXB 8834   0-7975
XXB 8835
XXB 8836   0-7976
XXB 8837

301/19-24 june 1941/telefunken sessions in berlin
singakademie
eugen jochum/*joseph kailberth
mozart symphony no 41 in c k551 "jupiter"
25893	SK 3333
25894	
25895	SK 3334
25896	
25897	SK 3335
25898	
25899	SK 3336
25900	

dvorak violin concerto in a minor op 53
with georg kulenkampff, violin
25925	SK 3237/ultraphon G 18033
25926	
25927	SK 3238/ultraphon G 18034
25028	
25929	SK 3239/ultraphon G 18035
25930	
25931	SK 3240/ultraphon G 18036
25932	

lp: HT 26/LGX 66020/GMA 101/capitol P 8052
cd: teldec 9031 764432

*bruch violin concerto no 1 in g minor op 26
with georg kulenkampff, violin
25933	SK 3172
25943	
25935	SK 3173
25936	
25937	SK 3174
25938	

cd: teldec 9031 764432/alta nova AN 1

302/3-4 july 1941/odeon sessions in berlin
hermann abendroth
brahms symphony no 1 in c minor op 68
XXB 8842   0-9122
XXB 8843
XXB 8844   0-9123
XXB 8845
XXB 8846   0-9124
XXB 8847
XXB 8848   0-9125
XXB 8849
XXB 8850   0-9126
XXB 8851
XXB 8852   0-9127
XXB 8853
cd: tahra TAH 102

303/27-29 september 1941/grammophon sessions in berlin
alte-jakob-strasse studios
carl schuricht
beethoven symphony no 3 in e flat op 55 "eroica"

1629	67793
1630	
1631	67794
1632	
1633	67795
1634	
1635	67796
1636	
1637	67797
1644	
1645	67798
1646	

lp: decca (usa) DL 9524

cd: deutsche grammophon 453 8042/

shinseido (japan) SGR 6001-6005 -

304/24-27 october 1941/grammophon sessions in berlin alte-jakob-strasse studios

bruno kittel

mozart requiem k626

with bruno-kittel-chor/tilla briem, soprano/gertrud freimuth, contralto/walther ludwig, tenor/fred drissen, bass

1694	67731
1695	
1696	67732
1697	
1698	67733
1699	
1700	67734
1701	
1702	67735
1703	
1704	67736
1705	
1706	67737
1707	
1708	67738
1709	
1710	67739

cd: deutsche grammophon 459 0042

305/30 october 1941/electrola sssions in berlin philharmonie
hans knappertsbusch
komzak bad'ner madeln waltz
2RA 5222   DB 7710
2RA 5223
cd: preiser 90236/tahra TAH 311-312

haydn symphony no 94 in g "surprise"
2RA 5224   DB 5671
2RA 5225
2RA 5226   DB 5672
2RA 5227
2RA 5228   DB 5673
2RA 5229
cd: preiser 90121/music and arts CD 897

306/7 november 1941/telefunken session in berlin singakademie
georg schumann
georg schumann drei deutsche tänze
26151   unpublished
26152
26253   unpublished
26154

307/14-16 december 1941/acetates from reichsrundfunk recording in berlin philharmonie
wilhelm furtwängler
bruckner symphony no 4 in e flat "romantic"
lp: japan AT 11-12
cd: delta (japan) DCCA 0001/japanese
furtwängler centre WFHC 018-020
there are many gaps in the music when acetates were changed

308/15-17 february 1942/reichsrundfunk recordings in berlin philharmonie
wilhelm furtwängler
strauss don juan
lp: discocorp RR 476
cd: deutsche grammophon 427 7822/427 7732/471 2942/
russian compact disc RCD 25008/melodiya MEL 10 00717/
music and arts CD 829/documents 20.3090/20.3093/223 508/
chibas restorations 1120/french furtwängler society SWF 031-032

strauss orchesterlieder: waldseligkeit; liebeshymnus; verführung; winterliebe
with peter anders, tenor
lp: melodiya M10 41233-41234/french furtwängler society SWF 7906/
discocorp IGI 382/nippon columbia OZ 7603/arabesque AR 8082/
cetra FE 41
cd: priceless D 18355/arabesque Z 6082/melodiya M10 00723/
russian compact disc RCD 25014/danye LYS 203/music and arts CD 829/
tahra FURT 201-202/FURT 1038-1039/chibas restorations 1110

309/26 february 1942/deutsche wochenschau film footage in berlin aeg factory (werkkonzert)
wilhelm furtwängler
wagner die meistersinger von nürnberg overture
lp: french furtwängler society SWF 8801-8803/japan AT 09-10/W 22-23
cd: tahra FURT 1036-1037/chibas restorations 1121-1124/
archipel ARPCD 0261
vhs video: bel canto society BCS 0052
dvd: arthaus 101 453

310/1-3 march 1942/reichsrundfunk recording in berlin philharmonie
wilhelm furtwängler
schumann piano concerto in a minor op 54
with walter gieseking, piano
lp: melodiya M10 36605-36606/everest SDBR 8434/discocorp IGI 348/
nippon columbia OZ 7596/french furtwängler society SWF 7701
cd: melodiya MEL 10 00719/russian compact disc RCD 25010/
deutsche grammophon 427 7792/427 7732/471 2942/dante
LYS 196/arlecchino ARL 151-152/opus kura OPK 7012/chibas
restorations 1119/pristine audio PASC 347/andante AN 2090

311/11-12 march 1942/electrola sessions in philharmonie
hans knappertsbusch
brahms symphony no 3 in f op 90

2RA 5433 unpublished
2RA 5434
2RA 5435 unpublished
2RA 5436
2RA 5437 unpublished
2RA 5438
2RA 5439 unpublished
2RA 5440
2RA 5441 unpublished
lp: discocorp IGI 383
cd: preiser 90121

liszt les preludes

2RA 5442 DB 5691
2RA 5443
2RA 5444 DB 5692
2RA 5445
lp: emi RLS 768/1C137 54095-54099
cd: emi CDF 300 012/preiser 90976/tahra TAH 311-312

312/22-24 march 1943/reichsrundfunk recording in berlin philharmonie
wilhelm furtwängler
beethoven symphony no 9 in d minor op 125 "choral"
with bruno-kittel-chor/tilla briem, soprano/elisabeth höngen, contralto/peter anders, tenor/rudolf watzke, bass
lp: melodiya D 010851-010854/M 10 10851 009/unicorn UNI 100-101/vox turnabout TV 4346-4347/TV 4353-4354/ french furtwängler society SWF 7003-7004/nippon columbia DXM 105-106/everest SDBR 3241/
emi 3C153 53810-53816M
cd: priceless D 13256/french furtwängler society SWF 891/ music and arts CD 653/arkadia CDWFE 357/melodiya MEL 10 00715/russian compact disc RCD 25006/ documents LV 919-920/historical performers HP 6/ dante LYS 071/grammofono AB 78581/tahra FURT 1004-1007/FURT 1036-1037/opus kura OPK 7003/ chibas restorations 1106

313/7 april 1942/telefunken session in berlin philharmonie
wilhelm furtwängler
bruckner symphony no 7: second movement
26378   SK 3230/ultraphon 922264
26379
26380   SK 3231/ultraphon 922265
26381
26382   SK 3232/ultraphon 922266
26383
lp: rococo 2014/japan 1101-1102/AT 11-12/discocorp RR 457/
french furtwängler society SWF 7702/SWF 8801-8802
cd: teldec 9031 764352/french furtwängler society SWF 963/
dante LYS 106-107/music and arts CD 954/naxos 8.111000/
tahra FURT 1004-1007/FURT 1099-1100/andromeda
ANDRCD 5008/japanese furtwängler society WFJ 17/
chibas restorations 1114

314/19 april 1942/decelith discs taken from reichsrundfunk recording in berlin philharmonie
wilhelm furtwängler
beethoven symphony no 9 in d minor op 125 "choral"
with bruno-kittel-chor/erna berger, soprano/gertrud pitzinger, contralto/helge rosvaenge, tenor/rudolf watzke, bass
cd: archipel ARPCD 0270
final bars and concluding applause also filmed for deutsche wochenschau but with the sound taken from the 22-24 march performance (session no. 312)

315/20-23 may 1942/newsreel film recording of werkkonzert in paris (fragmentary)
clemens krauss
schubert symphony no 8 in b minor d759 "unfinished"
dvd: dreamlife (japan) DVLC 1009

316/17-22 august 1942/grammophon sessions in berlin alte-jakob-strasse studios
carl schuricht
beethoven symphony no 6 in f op 68 "pastoral"
1982	68194
1983	
1984	68195
1985	
1986	68196
1987	
1988	68197
1989	
1990	68198
1991	
1992	68199

cd: shinseido (japan) SGR 6001-6005

mozart symphony no 34 in c k338
2005	68215
2006	
2007	68216
2008	
2009	68217

cd: dante LYS 178

317/24 august-1 september 1942/grammophon sessions in berlin alte-jakob-strasse studios
bruno kittel
bach matthäus-passion bwv244
with bruno-kittel-chor/tilla briem, soprano/gusta hammer, contralto/walther ludwig, tenor/hans hermann nissen, baritone/
fred drissen, bass

1906	67951/fonit 96101
1907	
1908	67952/fonit 96102
1909	
1910	67953/fonit 96103
1911	
1912	67954/fonit 96104
1913	
1914	67955/fonit 96105
1915	
1916	67956/fonit 96106
1917	
1918	67957/fonit 96107
1919	
1920	67958/fonit 96108
1921	
1922	67959/fonit 96109
1923	
1924	67960/fonit 96110
1925	
1926	67961/fonit 96111
1927	

317/august-september 1942/grammophon sessions/concluded

1928	67962/fonit 96112
1929	
1930	67963/fonit 96113
1931	
1932	67964/fonit 96114
1933	
1934	67965/fonit 96115
1935	
1936	67966/fonit 96116
1937	
1938	67967/fonit 96117
1939	
1940	67968/fonit 96118

318/15-16 october and 12 december 1942/electrola sessions in berlin philharmonie

hans knappertsbusch

pfitzner palestrina act one prelude
2RA 5701   DB 7677
2RA 5702
cd: preiser 90260/tahra TAH 311-312

weber-berlioz aufforderung zum tanz
2RA 5713   DB 7647
2RA 5714
cd: preiser 90260/tahra TAH 311-312

319/21 october 1942/grammophon session in berlin alte-jakob-strasse studios
herbert von karajan
johann strauss der zigeunerbaron overture
1975   67997
1976
cd: deutsche grammophon 423 5312/423 5252/459 0012/ 459 0652/477 6237/unlimited classics HDNC 0017/ pristine audio PACO 070

johann strauss die fledermaus overture
1977   68043
1978
cd: deutsche grammophon 423 5282/423 5252/477 6237/ unlimited classics HDNC 0017/pristine audio PACO 070
this item was incorrectly dated december 1943

320/25-28 october 1942/reichsrundfunk recordings in berlin philharmonie
wilhelm furtwängler
schumann cello concerto
with tibor de machula, cello
lp: melodiya M10 42555-42558/french furtwängler society SWF 8201-8202/discocorp RR 538/nippon columbia OZ 7596
cd: melodiya MEL 10 00721/russian compact disc RCD 25012/ dante LYS 196/deutsche grammophon 427 7792/427 7732/ 471 2942/arlecchino ARL 151-152/chibas restorations

320/25-28 october 1942/reichsrundfunk recordings/
concluded
bruckner symphony no 5 in b flat
lp: melodiya M10 42555-42558/french furtwängler society
SWF 8203-8204/discocorp RR 538/nippon columbia OZ 7600
cd: bella musica BMF 967/melodiya MEL 10 00714/russian
compact disc RCD 25005/deutsche grammophon 427 7742/
427 7732/471 2942/dante LYS 108/music and arts CD 538/
german furtwängler society WFG 2011/opus kura OPK 7013/
chibas restorations 1113

321/29 october 1942/telefunken session in berlin
singakademie
wilhelm furtwängler
gluck alceste overture
29753 SK 3266/T 122/GX 61008/capitol 81001
29754
45: UV 115
lp: LS 6025/capitol H 8130/japan JP 1101-1102/AT 09-10/
french furtwängler society SWF 7702/
melodiya M10 46683 000
cd: melodiya MEL 10 00724/russian compact disc RCD 25015/
dante LYS 117/documents 20.3090/20.3093/223 508/music
and arts CD 954/teldec 9031 764352/naxos 8.110994/
andromeda ABDRCD 5008/chibas restorations 1117

322/8-9 november 1942/reichsrundfunk recordings in berlin philharmonie

wilhelm furtwängler

brahms piano concerto no 2 in b flat op 83
with edwin fischer, piano
lp: melodiya D 09883-09884/unicorn UNI 102/french furtwängler society SWF 6901/nippon columbia DXM 108/emi 29 09701/ 1C149 53420-53426/2C153 53420-53426/3C153 53661-53669M
cd: deutsche grammophon 427 7782/427 7732/471 2942/ priceless D 14236/melodiya MEL 10 00724/dante LYS 046/ russian compact disc RCD 25015/music and arts CD 804/ testament SBT 1170/venezia V 1002/opus kura OPK 7018/ chibas restorations 1110/pristine audio PASC 347

wagner tristan prelude and liebestod
lp: melodiya M10 45949 008/french furtwängler society SWF 8801-8803
cd: melodiya MEL 10 00721/russian compact disc RCD 25012/ music and arts CD 730/tahra FURT 1004-1007/FURT 1036-1037/ archipel ARPCD 0261/chibas restorations 1121-1124

323/6-8 december 1942/reichsrundfunk recordings in berlin philharmonie

wilhelm furtwängler

heinz schubert hymnisches konzert for soprano, tenor, organ and orchestra
with erna beger, soprano/walther ludwig, tenor/fritz heitmann, organ
lp: melodiya M10 49723 000
cd: melodiya MEL 10 00725/russian compact disc RCD 25016/grammofono AB 78510/arkadia CDWFE 365

schubert symphony no 9 in c d944 "great"
lp: melodiya D 010033-010034/M10 10033 007/vox turnabout TV 4364/nippon columbia DXM 109/french furtwängler society SWF 7201
cd: priceless D 13272/bayer da capo 20 003/melodiya MEL 10 00723/russian compact disc RCD 25014/deutsche grammophon 427 7812/427 7732/471 2892/palladio PD 4176/dante LYS 114/music and arts CD 826/german furtwängler society TMK 017214/french furtwängler society SWF 031-032/japanese furtwängler society/opus kura OPK 7010/chibas restorations 1118/pristine audio PASC 253

324/november 1942-march 1943/sessions for the tobias-filmkunst feature film "philharmoniker" (directed by paul verhoeven), in which orchestra members participated

325/1942-1943/deutsche wochenschau film in berlin haus des rundfunks

eugen jochum

mozart le nozze di figaro overture
this footage can be viewed in the film "musikstadt berlin"

326/23 january and 31 march-1 april 1943/electrola sessions in berlin philharmonie

hans knappertsbusch

wagner siegfried idyll

2RA 5807   DB 7659
2RA 5808
2RA 5809   DB 7660
2RA 5810

beethoven symphony no 3 in e flat op 55 "eroica"

2RA 5913   DB 7666
2RA 5914
2RA 5915   DB 7667
2RA 5916
2RA 5917   DB 7668
2RA 5918
2RA 5919   DB 7669
2RA 5920
2RA 5921   DB 7670
2RA 5922
2RA 5923   DB 7671
2RA 5924

cd: preiser 90976

327/7-8 february 1943/reichsrundfunk recordings in berlin philharmonie
wilhelm furtwängler
sibelius violin concerto in d minor op 47
with georg kulenkampff, violin
lp: melodiya M10 45909 004/nippon columbia DXM 112/french furtwängler society SWF 8604/unicorn UNI 107
cd: melodiya MEL 10 00718/russian compact disc RCD 25009/ music and arts CD 799/chibas restorations 1125/ archipel ARPCD 0014

sibelius en saga
lp: melodiya M10 45909 004/french furtwängler society SWF 8604
cd: melodiya MEL 10 00718/russian compact disc RCD 25009/ deutsche grammophon 427 7832/427 7732/471 2942/ grammofono AB 78558/music and arts CD 799/french furtwängler society SWF 031-032/chibas restorations 1125

328/17 february 1943/reichsrundfunk recording in berlin philharmonie
karl böhm
max trapp violin concerto in a minor
ith erich röhn, violin
this recording remains unpblished

329/30 march 1943/reichsrundfunk recording in berlin philharmonie
hans knappertsbusch
mozart clarinet concerto k622
with alfred bürkner, clarinet
lp: longanesi GCL 48

330/18 april 1943/deutsche wochenschau film footage in berlin philharmonie
hans knappertsbusch
beethoven symphony no 9: concluding secion of final movement
with bruno-kittel-chor/erna berger, soprano/elisabeth höngen, contralto/torsten ralf, tenor/rudolf watzke, bass
cd: archipel ARPCD 5017
vhs video: bel canto society
dvd: bel canto society/arthaus musik 101 452

331/27-30 june 1943/reichsrundfunk recording in berlin philharmonie
wilhelm furtwängler
beethoven symphony no 4 in b flat op 60
lp: melodiya D 09083-09084/vox PL 7210/olympic 8120/8124/nippon columbia DXM 103/deutsche grammophon LPM 18 742/2535 813/ 2730 005/eterna 820 312/vox turnabout TV 4344/french furtwängler society SWF 7103/emi 1C153 53810-53816M
cd: melodiya MEL 10 00719/russian compact disc RCD 25010/ deutsche grammophon 427 7772/427 7732/471 2892/grammofono AB 78 502/dante LYS 072/music and arts CD 824/french furtwängler society SWF 011-013/opus kura OPK 7002/chibas restorations 1102
all lp editions of this recording contained only the first and second movements, to which were added the third and fourth movements from the reichsrundfunk recording without audience (session no. 332)

332/27-30 june 1943/reichsrundfunk recording without audience in berlin philharmonie
wilhelm furtwängler
beethoven symphony no 4 in b flat op 60
cd: french furtwängler society SWF 011-013/opus kura OPK 7107/ chibas restorations 1103

333/27-30 june 1943/reichsrundfunk recordings in berlin philharmonie
wilhelm furtwängler
beethoven symphony no 5 in c minor op 67
lp: melodiya D 05800-05801/M10 05800 009/unicorn UNI 106/
nippon columbia DXM 157/french furtwängler society SWF 7002/
vox turnabout TV 4353/TV 4361/TV 34478/ariston ARCL 13029/
emi 1C153 53810-53816M
cd: deutsche grammophon 427 7752/427 7732/471 2892/
melodiya MEL 10 00720/russian compact disc RCD 25011/
grammofono AB 78502/music and arts CD 824/dante LYS 065/
tahra FURT 272/FURT 1034-1035/FURT 1032-1033/emi 562 8752/
opus kura OPK 7001/chibas restorations 1102
emi 562 8752 is incorrectly dated february 1944

beethoven coriolan overture op 62
lp: melodiya D 09867-09868/M10 09867 006/discocorp SID 713/
nippon columbia DXM 103/french furtwängler society SWF 7002/
emi 1C153 53810-53816M
cd: deutsche grammophon 427 7802/427 7732/453 8042/
453 7002/471 2892/melodiya MEL 10 00718/russian compact disc
RCD 25009/documents 20.3090/20.3095/223 508/grammofono
AB 78502/dante LYS 064/music and arts CD 826/CD 942/tahra
FURT 1004-1007/chibas restorations 1103/german furtwängler
society TMK 017204/japanese furtwängler society WFJ 23/
opus kura OPK 7026

334/8 july 1943/reichsrundfunk recording in berlin
haus des rundfunks
eugen jochum
reger serenade in g op 95
lp: urania URLP 7052

335/31 october-3 november 1943/reichsrundfunk recordings
in berlin philharnomie
wilhelm furtwängler
pepping symphony no 2 in f minor
lp: melodiya M10 49721 000/japan AT 13-14
cd: melodiya MEL 10 00725/russian compact discs RCD 25016/arkadia CDWFE 365/grammofono AB 78510

beethoven piano concerto no 4 in g op 58
with conrad hansen, piano
lp: unicorn UNI 105/french furtwängler society SWF 7005R/nippon columbia DXM 104/deutsche grammophon 2535 807/melodiya M10 46067 003/emi 3C153 53010-53016M
cd: melodiya MEL 10 00771/russian compact disc RCD 25002/french furtwängler society SWF 941/SWF 941R/arkadia CDWFE 365/music and arts CD 839/tahra FURT 1034-1035/dreamlife DCLA 7007/chibas restorations 1101

beethoven symphony no 7 in a op 92
lp: melodiya D 027779-027780/vox turnabout TV 34509/unicorn WFS 8/french furtwängler society SWF 7105/olympic OL 8120/OL 8129/intercord 120 924/emi 1C153 53810-53816M
cd: deutsche grammophon 417 7752/427 7732/471 2892/melodiya MEL 10 00713/russian compact disc RCD 25004/french furtwängler society SWF 941/SWF 941R/opus kura OPK 7002/dreamlife DCLA 7007/chibas restorations 1104

336/5 november 1943/reichsrundfunk recording in berlin
eugen jochum
mozart symphony no 33 in b flat k319
lp: urania URSP 101

337/13-16 november 1943/reichsrundfunk recordings in berlin philhamonie
wilhelm furtwängler
bruckner symphony no 6 in a
lp: melodiya M10 47465 005/japan W 28-29/french furtwängler society SWF 8801-8803
cd: melodiya MEL 10 00720/russian compact disc RCD 25011/ dante LYS 105-107/music and arts CD 805/french furtwängler society SWF 963/emi 566 2102/chibas restorations 1114/ tahra FURT 1004-1007
first movement is missing from this recording

schumann cello concerto: third movement
with pierre fournier, cello
cd: tahra FURT 1008-1011/dante LYS 196/japanese furtwängler society WFJ 23/chibas restorations 1119

strauss till eulenspiegels lustige streiche
45: deutsche grammophon EPL 30 589/eterna 520 439
lp: deutsche grammophon LPM 18 960/2721 202/2535 816/ 2548 719/royale 1259/gramophone (usa) 2097
cd: deutsche grammophon 417 7832/427 7732/439 8372/ 471 2942/music and arts CD 829/french furtwänglersociety SWF 031-032/chibas restorations 1120
LPM 18 960 and 2548 719 were incorrectly dated

338/12-15 december 1943/reichsrundfunk recordings in berlin philharmonie
wilhelm furtwängler
brahms haydn variations op 56a
lp: melodiya D 010851-010854/M10 10851 009/unicorn UNI 100-101/ everest SDBR 3252/nippon columbia DXM 104/OS 7076/french furtwängler society SWF 8203-8204/emi 3C153 53661-53669M
cd: priceless D 14236/melodiya MEL 10 00722/russian compact disc RCD 25013/magic talent MT 48059/grammofono AB 78594/ dante LYS 049/music and arts CD 805/CD 941/opus kura OPK 7010/tahra FURT 1038-1039/chibas restorations 1112

brahms piano concerto no 2 in b flat op 83
with adrian aeschbacher, piano
lp: melodiya M10 45921 009/french furtwängler society SWF 8502
cd: french furtwängler society SWF 951-952/music and arts CD 941/ dante LYS 049/tahra FURT 1004-1007/FURT 1938-1039/ chibas restorations 1109

brahms symphony no 4 in e minor op 98
lp: melodiya D 09867-09868/M10 09867 006/rococo 2013/nippon columbia DXM 107/OW 7823/discocorp RR 418/ emi 1C153 53661-53669M
cd: melodiya MEL 10 00722/russian compact disc RCD 25013/ magic talent MT 48059/arkadia CDWFE 365/french furtwängler society SWF 951-952/grammofono AB 78594/dante LYS 048/ music and arts CD 804/CD 941/tahra FURT 1038-1039/opus kura OPK 7012/pristine audio PASC 344/chibas restoraions 1112

339/9-12 january 1944/reichsrundfunk recordings in berlin philharmonie

wilhelm furtwängler

beethoven violin concerto in d op 61
with erich röhn, violin
lp: melodiya M10 40929-40920/french furtwängler society SWF 7901/ discocorp IGI 364
cd: melodiya MEL 10 00716/russian compact disc RCD 25007/ as-disc AS 331-332/documents 20.3090/20.3095/223 508/deutsche grammophon 427 7802/427 7732/471 2892/french furtwängler society SWF 011-013/opus kura OPK 7017/chibas restorations 1101

strauss sinfonia domestica
lp: melodiya M10 40961-40962/french furtwängler society SWF 7902/ discocorp IGI 364/arabesque AR 8082/cetra FE 41
cd: arabesque Z 6082/as-disc AS 331-332/melodiya MEL 10 00717/ russian compact disc RCD 25008/deutsche grammophon 427 7822/ 427 7732/471 2942/dante LYS 203/magic talent MT 48090/ arlecchino ARL 111-112/chibas restorations 1120

340/7-8 february 1944/reichsrundfunk recordings in berlin staatsoper unter den linden
wilhelm furtwängler
mozart symphony no 39 in e flat k543
lp: melodiya M10 46005 000/french furtwängler society SWF 8601
cd: melodiya MEL 10 00716/russian compact disc RCD 25007/ dante LYS 117/iron needle IN 1340/deutsche grammophon 427 7762/427 7732/471 2892/chibas restorations 1117

handel concerto grosso in d minor op 6 no 10
lp: melodiya M10 46005 000/french furtwängler society SWF 8601
cd: melodiya MEL 10 00721/russian compact disc RCD 23012/ dante LYS 250/deutsche grammophon 427 7772/427 7732/ 471 2892/chibas restorations 1117

341/10 march 1944/reichsrundfunk recording in berliner dom
hans knappertsbusch
handel concerto grosso in d op 6 no 5
lp: discocorp RR 536
cd: music and arts CD 4897/documents 205.229/ archipel ARPCD 0102

342/20-21 march 1944/reichsrundfunk recordings in berlin
staatsoper unter den linden
wilhelm furtwängler
weber der freischütz overture
lp: melodiya M10 41233-41234/french furtwängler
society SWF 8203-8204/japan AT 09-10
cd: deutsche grammophon 427 7812/427 7732/471 2892/melodiya
MEL 10 00712/russian compact disc RCD 25003/music and arts CD 826/
french furtwängler society SWF 031-032/chibas restorations 1117

ravel daphnis et chloe second suite
lp: melodiya M10 45949 008/french furtwängler society SWF 8801-8803
cd: deutsche grammophon 427 7832/427 7732/471 2892/melodiya
MEL 10 00712/russian compact disc RCD 25003/dante LYS 124/
german furtwängler society TMK 017204/chibas restorations 1125/
berliner philharmoniker BPH 0604

beethoven symphony no 6 in f op 68 "patoral"
lp: melodiya D 02777-02778/M10 02777 004/rococo 2077/nippon
columbia DXM 155/OZ 7586/french furtwängler society SWF 7104R/
discocorp RR 412
cd: french furtwängler society SWF 901/melodiya MEL 10 00712/
russian compact disc RCD 25003/documents 20.3090/20.3095/
223 508/dante LYS 064/music and arts WFSA 2001/CD 824/
CD 942/tahra FURT 1004-1007/FURT 1036-1037/opus kura
OPK 7001/chibas restorations 1104

343/26 march 1944/reichsrundfunk recording without audience in berlin haus des rundfunks
hans knappertsbusch
brahms symphony no 2 in d op 73
lp: discocorp RR 536
cd: tahra TAH 320-322/arlecchino ARLA 98-102/archipel ARPCD 0050/urania SP 4207

344/22-23 may 1944/film footage in granada during orchestra tour of spain and portugal
hans knappertsbusch
filmed repertoire included beethoven symphony no 5, tchaikovsky symphony no 6 and debussy prelude a l'apres-midi d'un faune, surviving fragments of which can be viewed in the film "botschafter der musik" and in the dvd published by arthaus musik 101 452 ("das reichsorchester")

345/july 1944/reichsrundfunk recordings without audience during temporary evacuation of the orchestra to baden-baden
robert heger
brahms piano concerto no 2: first and second movements
with walter gieseking, piano
cd: arbiter 103

schumann piano concerto in a minor op 54
with walter gieseking, piano
lp: discocorp IGI 363
cd: tahra TAH 195

345/july 1944/reichsrundfunk in baden-baden/concluded
grieg piano concerto in a minor op 16
with walter gieseking, piano
lp: discocorp IGI 348
cd: tahra TAH 195/music and arts CD 925
this recording was published on a number of other labels with the incorrect attribution of wilhelm furtwängler as conductor

346/8-9 september 1944/reichsrundfunk recordings without audience during temporary evacuation of the orchestra in baden-baden
hans knappertsbusch
bruckner symphony no 4 in e flat "romantic"
lp: discocorp IGI 383
cd: music and arts CD 249/CD 1028/iron needle IN 1344/grammofono AB 78563/preiser 90226/tahra TAH 320-322/documents 205 229/ 204 351/cantus classics 500 190/archipel ARPCD 0044/urania URN 22225/andromeda ANDRCD 9010
some editions were incorrectly dated march 1944

brahms symphony no 3 in f op 90
lp: discocorp IGI 383/melodiya D 06429-06430
cd: arlecchino ARLA 98-102/tahra TAH 320-322/green hill GH 0006-0007/documents 222 334/archipel ARPCD 0050
lp editions were incorrectly dated march 1942

347/20-22 september 1944/reichsrundfunk recordings
without audience in berlin haus des rundfunks
hermann abendroth
wagner a faust overture
cd: radio years RY 66-67

mozart violin concerto no 3 in g k216
with erich röhn, violin
cd: tahra TAH 192-193

gluck iphigenie in aulis overture
lp: urania URLP 7028
cd: tahra TAH 139

gluck orfeo ed euridice: dance of the furies and dance of the blessed spirits
cd: tahra TAH 192-193

gluck orfeo ed euridice: che faro senza euridice?
with margarete klose, contralto/*sung in german*
cd: tahra TAH 192-193

handel concerto grosso in g minor op 6 no 6
cd: tahra TAH 192-193

handel giulio cesare: v'adoro pupille
with margarete klose, contralto/*sung in german*
lp: eterna 820 922
cd: tahra TAH 192-193

348/7 october 1944/reichsrundfunk recordings without audience in berlin haus des rundfunks
wilhelm furtwängler
mozart symphony no 39 in e flat k543
lp: deutsche grammophon LPM 18 725/LPM 18 856/KL 27-32/2535 828/ 2721 202/2730 005/2740 260/heliodor 88 007/eterna 720 158
cd: deutsche grammophon 431 8732/439 8322/477 0062/dante LYS 246/ documents 20.3090/20.3091/223 508/music and arts CD 954/ opus kura OPK 7018/french furtwängler society SWF 991
most editions have been incorrectly dated 1942-1943

bruckner symphony no 9 in d minor
lp: deutsche grammophon LPM 18 854/KL 27-32/2730 005/2740 201/ heliodor 88 019/eterna 820 380
cd: music and arts CD 730/dante LYS 110/grammofono AB 78696-78697/ deutsche grammophon 445 4182/chibas restorations 1116/ pristine audio PASC 251

349/13 october 1944/reichsrundfunk recording without audience in berlin haus des rundfunks
hermann abendroth
beethoven piano concerto no 5 in e flat op 73 "emperor"
with elly ney, piano
cd: tahra TAH 192-193

350/15 october 1944/reichsrundfunk recording in berlin
staatsoper unter den linden
eugen jochum
franz schmidt variations on a theme by beethoven
with friedrich wührer, piano
cd: tahra TAH 384

351/7-30 november 1944/odeon sessions in berlin
fritz lehmann
bruch violin concerto no 1 in g minor
with gerhard taschner, violin
XXB 9481   unpublished
XXB 9482
XXB 9483   unpublished
XXB 9484
XXB 9485   unpublished
XXB 9486

mozart symphony no 39 in e flat k543
XXB 9491   unpublished
XXB 9492
XXB 9493   unpublished
XXB 9494
XXB 9495   unpublished
XXB 9496

352/3 december 1944/reichsrundfunk recording in berlin staatsoper unter den linden
fritz zaun
liszt tasso lamento e trionfo
lp: urania URLP 7091

353/12 december 1944/reichsrundfunk recording in berlin admiralspalast
wilhelm furtwängler
schubert symphony no 8 "unfinished": first movement
cd: tahra FURT 1006/chibas restorations 1118/
french furtwängler society SWF 031-032

354/16 december 1944/reichsrundfunk recording in berlin haus des rundfunks
hermann abendroth
bruch violin concerto no 1 in g minor
with gerhard taschner, violin
cd: tahra TAH 192-193/archiphon ARC 126

354a/1944/reichsrundfunk recordings in berlin
ernst schrader
dvorak symphony no 7 in d minor op 70; weber clarinet concertino
with alfred bürkner, clarinet
lp: urania URLP 7015/classics club 119
cd: crq editions CRQCD 333

355/31 december 1944/reichsrundfunk recording in berlin admiralspalast
arthur rother
weber der freischütz overture
lp: avon AV 3014

356/1944-1945/deutsche wochenschau film footage in berlin staatsoper unter den linden
hans knappertsbusch
liszt les preludes; beethoven symphony no 3 "eroica"
extracts from these performances can be viewed in the films "botschafter der musik" and "musikstadt berlin"

357/14 january 1945/reichsrundfunk recording in berlin admiralspalast
eugen jochum
beethoven symphony no 5 in c minor op 67
cd: tahra TAH 229

358/23 january 1945/reichsrundfunk recording in berlin admiralspalast
wilhelm furtwängler
brahms symphony no 1: fourth movement
lp: french furtwängler society SWF 8801-8803/japan AT 13-14
cd: refrain DR 91 0004/french furtwängler society SWF 951-952/ music and arts CD 805/CD 941/dante LYS 048/LYS 204/tahra FURT 1004-1007/japanese furtwängler centre WFHC 024/ chibas restorations 1109
concert was interrupted by power failure following an air-raid

359/1945/film footage in berlin maxim-gorki-theater
john bitter
tchaikovsky serenade for strings: rehearsal extracts
parts of this footage can be viewed in the film "musikstadt berlin"

359a/17 and 30 june 1945/berliner rundfunk recordings without audience in haus des rundfunks
leo borchard
glazunov stenka rasin; weber oberon overture; tchaikovsky romeo and juliet
cd: tahra TAH 520
glazunov item was also published in various lp and cd editions with the incorrect attribution of wilhelm furtwängler as conductor

360/18-21 november 1945/berliner rundfunk recordings without audience in berlin haus des rundfunks
sergiu celibidache
dvorak cello concerto in b minor op 104
with tibor de machula, cello
cd: pearl GEMMCD 9198/grammofono AB 78730/
music and arts CD 1079/audite 21.423

brahms symphony no 4 in e minor op 98
cd: tahra TAH 271/myto 981.H009/grammofono AB 78774-78775/
music and arts CD 1079/audite 21.423

361/20 january 1946/berliner rundfunk recordings without audience in berlin haus des rundfunks
sergiu celibidache
saint-saens samson et dalilah: mon coeur s'ouvre a ta voix; hugo wolf orchesterlieder: über nacht; denk es o seele!; gebet; anakreons grab; gesang weylas
with margarete klose, contralto
cd: tahra TAH 273 (saint-saens)/audite 21.423

362/25 march 1946/berliner rundfunk recording without audience in berlin haus des rundfunks
sergiu celibidache
tchaikovsky romeo and juliet fantasy overture
cd: music and arts CD 1079/audite 21.423

363/6 july 1946/berliner rundfunk recordings without audience in berlin haus des rundfunks
sergiu celibidache
gliere concerto for coloratura soprano and orchestra
with erna berger, soprano
cd: grammofono AB 78774-78775/myto 981 H.009/audiophile APL 101.525/music and arts CD 1079/audite 21.423

prokofiev symphony no 1 "classical"
cd: music and arts CD 1079/audite 21.423

364/1 september 1946/berliner rundfunk recording without audience in berlin haus des rundfunks
sergiu celibidache
prokofiev romeo and juliet: second suite
cd: music and arts CD 1079/audite 21.423

365/28 september 1946/berliner rundfunk recording without audience in berlin haus des rundfunks
sergiu celibidache
haydn symphony no 104 in d "london"
cd: audiophile 101.525/music and arts CD 1079/audite 21.423

366/10 november 1946/berliner rundfunk recordings without audience in berlin haus des rundfunks
sergiu celibidache
britten sinfonia da requiem; beethoven leonore no 3 overture
cd: tahra TAH 273/music and arts CD 1079/audite 21.423

debussy trois nocturnes: fetes
cd: music and arts CD 1079/audite 21.423

367/8 december 1946/berliner rundfunk recording without audience in berlin haus des rundfunks
sergiu celibidache
tiessen vorspiel zu einem drama
cd: audite 21.423

368/21 december 1946/berliner rundfunk recording
without audience in berlin haus des rundfunks
sergiu celibidache
shostakovich symphony no 7 "leningrad"
lp: urania URLP 601
cd: theorema TH 121-122/grammofono AB 78685/
audopphile 101.106
this was the first german performance of the symphony: public
premiere followed on 22 december in berlin admiralspalast;
filmed rehearsal fragments can be viewed in the film
"musikstadt berlin"

369/19 april 1947/berliner rundfunk recording without
audience in berlin haus des rundfunks
sergiu celibidache
berlioz le carnaval romain overture
cd: music and arts CD 1079/audite 21.423

370/25 may 1947/rias berlin recordings in titania palast
wilhelm furtwängler
beethoven symphony no 5; symphony no 6 "pastoral"
lp: cetra FE 32
cd: cetra CDE 1014/rodolphe RPC 32422-32424/german furtwängler
society TMK 08080/music and arts CD 789/CD 942 (no 5)/bellaphon
689 22003 (no 6)/tahra FURT 1016/FURT 2002-2004/dante
LYS 198 (no 5)/chibas restorations 1126/audite 21.403/
private edition vienna
this was furtwängler's first post-war concert in berlin

371/27 may 1947/berliner rundfunk recordings without audience in berlin haus des rundfunks
wilhelm furtwängler
beethoven egmont overture
lp: deutsche grammophon LPM 18 724/LPM 18 859/004 279/2535 810/ 2721 202/2730 005/2740 260/heliodor 88 008
cd: deutsche grammophon 439 8322/477 0062/nuova era 013.6313/ 013.6300/french furtwängler society SWF 011-013/chibas restorations 1105

beethoven symphony no 5 in c minor op 67
lp: deutsche grammophon LPM 18 724/2535 810/2721 202/2730 005/ 2740 260/heliodor 88 008/heliodor (usa) H 25078/HS 25078/eterna 820 280
cd: deutsche grammophon 439 8322/474 7282/bellaphon 689 22003/ french furtwängler society SWF 011-013/chibas restorations 1105

372/31 august 1947/berliner rundfunk recordings without audience in berlin haus des rundfunks
sergiu celibidache
berlioz le corsaire overture; debussy la mer
cd: tahra TAH 290/audite 21.423

shostakovich symphony no 9 in e flat
cd: audiophile APL 101.525/tahra TAH 290/audite 21.423

strauss till eulenspiegels lustige streiche
cd: music and arts CD 1079/tahra TAH 290/audite 21.423

373/14 september 1947/rehearsal recording in berlin
haus des rundfunks
wilhelm furtwängler
brahms symphony no 2: second movement
lp: french furtwängler society SWF 062-063
cd: tahra FURT 1008-1011

374/16 september 1947/berliner rundfunk recordings
without audience in berlin-dahlem gemeindehaus
wilhelm furtwängler
hindemith symphonic metamorphoses on themes of weber
lp: deutsche grammophon LPM 18 857/2535 164
cd: dante LYS 212/deutsche grammophon 474 0302/
french furtwängler society SWF 001-002

strauss don juan
lp: deutsche grammophon LPM 18 960/2535 616/2548 719/2721 202
cd: deutsche grammophon 439 8372/474 0302/arlecchino ARL 111-112

375/28 september 1947/rias berlin recordings in titania palast
wilhelm furtwängler
mendelssohn ein sommernachtstraum overture
lp: cetra FE 35
cd: german furtwängler society TMK 08080/tahra FURT 1020/
audite 21.403

beethoven violin concerto in d op 61
with yehudi menuhin, violin
lp: cetra FE 1
cd: cetra CDE 1013/german furtwängler society TMK 08080/tahra
FURT 1020/music and arts CD 708/audite 21.403

376/27 october 1947/berliner rundfunk recording in titania palast
wilhelm furtwängler
strauss metamorphosen
lp: deutsche grammophon LPM 18 857/2535 816/2548 719
cd: dante LYS 212/arlecchino ARL 111-112/music and arts CD 719/ deutsche grammophon 477 0062/french furtwängler society SWF 001-002

377/28 january-6 february 1948/columbia sessions in berlin zwölf-apostel-kirche
john bitter
berlioz le carnaval romain overture
CRX 300   LWX 386
CRX 301

mendelssohn ein sommernachtstraum: overture and nocturne
CRX 302   unpublished
CRX 306
CRX 304   unpublished
CRX 305

378/1 february 1948/berliner rundfunk recording without audience in berlin haus des rundfunks
eugen jochum
mozart symphony no 33 in b flat k319
cd: tahra TAH 470-473

379/3-12 february 1948/electrola sessions in berlin
zwölf-apostel-kirche
sergiu celibidache
prokofiev symphony no 1 "classical"
2RA 6123   DB 11508/C 3729
2RA 6126
2RA 6127   DB 11509/C 3730
2RA 6128
lp: victor LBC 1009/emi RLS 768/1C137 54095-54099
cd: emi CDF 300 012/569 7432

tchaikovsky capriccio italien
2RA 6129   unpublished
2RA 6130
2RA 6131   unpublished
2RA 6132

mendelssohn violin concerto in e minor op 64
with siegfried borries, violin
2RA 6135   DB 11516
2RA 6136
2RA 6137   DB 11517
2RA 6138
2RA 6139   DB 11518
2RA 6140
2RA 6141   DB 11519
45: victor WBC 1021/WBC 1049
lp: HZEL 700/victor LBC 1021/LBC 1049

380/19-21 february 1948/rehearsal recording in berlin titania palast
wilhelm furtwängler
furtwängler symphony no 2: second movement
cd: refrain (japan) DR 92 0031
public premiere performance of the symphony took place in berlin admiralspast on 22-23 february 1948

381/20 march 1948/rias berlin recording without audience in jesus-christus-kirche
sergiu celibidache
debussy jeux
cd: music and arts CD 734/berliner philharmoniker BPH 0605/audite 21.423

382/11-19 april 1948/rias berlin recordings in titania palast
artur rother/*leopold ludwig
tchaikovsky violin concerto; *beethoven violin concerto
with gerhard taschner, violin
lp: royale 1265 and 1307 respectively
these lps, originating from the record corporation of america, carried the various pseudonyms "fritz malachowsky/jan balachowsky/berlin symphony orchestra/joseph balzer/gerd rubahn"; they were listed in the world's encyclopedia of recorded music (second supplement) but opinions are divided as to whether they are genuine taschner performances

383/23 june 1948/electrola session in berlin zwölf-apostel-kirche
leopold ludwig
schumann symphony no 3: first movement
2RA 6164   unpublished
2RA 6165

384/22 october 1948/sender freies berlin recordings without audience in berlin-dahlem gemeindehaus
wilhelm furtwängler
bach orchestral suite no 3 in d bwv1068
lp: deutsche grammophon LPM 18 856/KL 27-32/2535 806
cd: deutsche grammophon 477 0062

brahms symphony no 4 in e minor op 98
cd: tahra FURT 1025/japanese furtwängler centre WFHC 003

385/24 october 1948/rias berlin recordings in titania palast
wilhelm furtwängler
bach orchestral suite no 3 in d bwv1068
lp: german furtwängler society F668.164-165
cd: german furtwängler society TMK 12681/music and arts CD 708/ tahra FURT 1026/audite 21.403

schubert symphony no 8 in b minor d759 "unfinished"
lp: vox turnabout TV 34478
cd: priceless D 13272/german furtwängler society TMK 12681/ audite 21.493

385/24 october 1948/rias berlin recordings/concluded
brahms symphony no 4 in e minor op 98
lp: hmv FALP 544/electrola E 90995/WALP 548/unicorn WFS 1/
emi 1C047 01147M/1C147 50336-50339M/1C149 53420-53426/
2C153 53420-53426/3C153 53661-53669M
cd: as-disc AS 331-332/virtuoso 269 9072/refrain DR 91 0004/
emi 252 3212/565 5132/907 8782/audite 21.403/
chibas restorations 1145
refrain edition incorrecly dated 22 october; 907 8782 incorrectly describes orchestra as wiener philharmoniker

386/3 november 1948/newsreel film footage of rehearsal in london empress hall
wilhelm furtwängler
brahms symphony no 4: fourth movement
cd: japanese furtwängler society WFJ 19
vhs video: teldec 4509 950383
dvd: teldec 4509 950386

387/7 march 1949/rias berlin recording in titania plast
sergiu celibidache
cherubini anacreon overture
cd: audiophile APL 101.524/audite 21.406

388/14 march 1949/sender freies berlin recording without audience in berlin-dahlem gemeindehaus
wilhelm furtwängler
bruckner symphony no 8 in c minor
cd: testament SBT 1143
previous lp editions purporting to contain this performance
(hmv FALP 850-851/electrola STE 91375-91378/SMVP 8057-8058/
emi 1C147 29231-29232/dante LYS 244) are considered to be a
conflation of the two performances on 14 and 15 march

389/15 march 1949/rias berlin recording in titania palast
wilhelm furtwängler
bruckner symphony no 8 in c minor
lp: rococo 2032/discocorp RR 457/nippon columbia OS 7091-7092
cd: arkadia CDWFE 356/palladio PD 4135/german furtwängler society MMS 9013/originals SH 854/dante LYS 245/music and arts CD 624/emi 566 2102/audite 21.403

390/9 may 1949/rias berlin recording without audience in jesus-christus-kirche
sergiu celibidache
busoni violin concerto
with siegfried borries, violin
cd: arkadia CDGI 734/audiophile APL 101.525/audite 21.406

rudi stephan musik für orchester
cd: audite 21.423

391/10 june 1949/hessischer rundfunk recording in wiesbaden staatstheater
wilhelm furtwängler
pfitzner palestrina three preludes
lp: rococo 2034/german furtwängler society F666.156-157/discocorp RR 457/cetra FE 26/nippon columbia OZ 7598-7599
cd: as-disc AS 370/tahra FURT 1021-1022

mozart symphony no 40 in g minor k550
lp: german furtwängler society F666.156-157/discocorp RR 395/ cetra FE 18/nippon columbia OZ 7598-7599
cd: cetra CDE 1015/CDE 3009/virtuoso 269 7352/tahra FURT 1021-1022

brahms symphony no 4 in e minor op 98
lp: german furtwängler society F666.157-158/discocorp RR 394/ nippon columbia OZ 7598-7599
cd: dante LYS 206/elaborations ELA 903/tahra FURT 1021-1022

392/4 september 1949/rias berlin recording in titania palast
sergiu celibidache
hindemith piano concerto
with gerhard puchelt, piano
cd: nuova era NE 6348-6349/urania URN 22101/audite 21.406

393/10 september 1949/rias berlin recordings without audience in jesus-christus-kirche
sergiu celibidache
milhaud suite symphonique: overture, nocturne and finale
cd: audite 21.423

394/12-15 september 1949/dg sessions in berlin
jesus-christus-kirche
ferenc fricsay
rossini italiana in algeri overture
01706   LVM 72 061
45: EPL 30 064
lp: LPEM 19 041/2535 717/2548 127
cd: 477 5908/479 3578/tahra TAH 454

johann strauss an der schönen blauen donau
01751   LVM 72 052
45: EPL 30 073
cd: 479 3578

johann and josef strauss perpetuum mobile
01944   L 62 870
45: NL 32 123
cd: 479 3578
coupled with matrix number 01960 (session no. 408)

tchaikovsky symphony no 5 in e minor op 64
01758   LVM 72 001/polydor (italy) RR 8187
01759
01760   LVM 72 002/polydor (italy) RR 8188
01761
01762   LVM 72 003/polydor (italy) RR 8189
01763
01764   LVM 72 004/polydor (italy) RR 8190
lp: LPM 18 021/2535 735/heliodor 89 627
cd: 459 0112/479 3578

395/18 october 1949/sender freies berlin recordings without audience in berlin-dahlem gemeindehaus
wilhelm furtwängler
beethoven leonore no 2 overture
lp: deutsche grammophon LPM 18 742/LPM 18 859/2535 807/
2730 005/heliodor 88 008/melodiya D 26585-26586
cd: deutsche grammophon 477 0062/chibas restorations 1130/
french furtwängler society SWF 011-013

karl höller cello concerto no 2
with ludwig hoelscher, cello
lp: cetra FE 31
cd: originals SH 834/french furtwängler society SWF 001-002

bruckner symphony no 7 in e
lp: HMV FALP 852-853/electrola STE 91375-91378/SMVP 8055-8056/
emi HQM 1169/F666.700/1C147 29229-29230
cd: dante LYS 214/emi 566 2062/chibas restorations 1129/french furtwängler society SWF 051/pristine audio

396/18-19 december 1949/rias berlin recordings in titania palast
wilhelm furtwängler
schumann manfred overture
lp: deutsche grammophon 2535 805
cd: deutsche grammophon 415 6612/427 4042/474 0302/virtuoso
269 7402/arlecchino ARL 151-152/audite 21.403

396/18-19 december 1949/rias recordings/concluded
brahms symphony no 3 in f op 90
lp: hmv FALP 543/electrola E 90994/WALP 547/unicorn WFS 4/
emi 1C027 01146M/1C147 50336-50339M/1C149 53420-53426/
2C153 53420-53426/3C153 53661-53669M
cd: virtuoso 269 9072/emi 252 3212/565 5132/907 8782/
audite 21.403
907 8782 incorrectly describes orchestra as wiener
philharmoniker and recording date as 8 december 1949

wolfgang fortner violin concerto
with gerhard taschner, violin
lp: cetra FE 31
cd: as-disc AS 370/german furtwängler society TMK 12681/
audite 21.403

wagner götterdämmerung: siegfrieds trauermarsch;
die meistersinger von nürnberg overture
lp: deutsche grammophon 2535 806/2721 113/2721 202/2740 260
cd: deutsche grammophon 415 6632/427 4062/439 8372/
474 0302/479 1148/archipel ARPCD 0261 (meistersinger)/
audite 21.403

397/1950/studio-made film performance against backdrop simulating ruins of the alte philharmonie
sergiu celibidache
beethoven egmont overture
lp: period SPL 716
dvd: teldec 4509 957103/4509 964383
footage can also be viewed in the film "botschafter der musik"

398/28 january 1950/rias berlin recordings without audience in titania palast
hans knappertsbusch
schubert symphony no 8 in b minor d759 "unfinished"
lp: melodram MEL 216
cd: tahra TAH 214-215/chaconne CHCD 1001/documents 222 334/audite 21.405

bruckner symphony no 9 in d minor
lp: longanesi GCL 56/melodram MEL 216
cd: music and arts CD 219/CD 1028/foyer CDS 16004/chaconne CHCD 1001/archipel ARPCD 0034/urania 22225/andromeda ANCRCD 9010/tahra TAH 207-208/audite 21.405

399/30 january 1950/rias berlin recordings in titania palast
hans knappertsbusch
schubert symphony no 8 in b minor d759 "unfinished";
bruckner symphony no 9 in d minor
cd: tahra TAH 417-418/audite 21.405

400/1 february 1950/rias berlin recordings in titania palast

hans knappertsbusch

nicolai die lustigen weiber von windsor overture
lp: musenkranz GMV 16
cd: arkadia CDGI 723/documents 205 229/archipel ARPCD 0120/
tahra TAH 214-215/audite 21.405

haydn symphony no 94 in g "surprise"
lp: longanesi GCL 62
cd: music and arts CD 4896/curcio CON 23/documents 222 334/
istituto discografico italiano IDIS 6362/archipel ARPCD 0120/
tahra TAH 214-215/audite 21.405

tchaikovsky casse noisette ballet suite
lp: musenkranz GMV 16
cd: archipel ARPCD 0120/tahra TAH 214-215/audite 21.405

johann strauss die fledermaus overture
lp: musenkranz GMV 16
cd: curcio CON 17/archipel ARPCD 0120/tahra TAH 214-215/
audite 21.405

johann and josef strauss pizzicato polka
lp: musenkranz GMV 16
cd: curcio CON 17/archipel ARPCD 0120/tahra TAH 214-215/
audite 21.405

komzak badner mad'ln waltz
lp: musenkranz GMV 16
cd: archipel ARPCD 0120/tahra TAH 214-215/audite 21.405

401/19-21 february 1950/rias berlin recordings without audience in jesus-christus-kirche
sergiu celibidache
haydn symphony no 104 in d "london"
lp: cetra LO 535
cd: arkadia CDGI 734/curcio CON 23/arlecchino ARLA 96/ nuova era NE 6348-6349/audite 21.423

tchaikovsky symphony no 2 in c minor "little russian"
lp: cetra LO 535
cd: arkadia CDGI 734/nuova era NE 2301-2302/audite 21.423

402/6 march 1950/rias berlin recordings without audience in jesus-christus-kirche
sergiu celibidache
mozart violin concerto no 5 in g k219
with lilia d'albore, violin
cd: arkadia CDGI 734/arlecchino ARLA 93/audite 21.423

stravinsky jeu de cartes
lp: cetra LO 535
cd: arkadia CDGI 734/nuova era NE 2301-2302/audite 21.423

403/6 april 1950/rias berlin recordings without audience in jesus-christus-kirche
sergiu celibidache
copland appalachian spring
cd: gewandhaus music circle CG 26-27/audiophile APL 101.524/ audite 21.423

barber capricorn concerto
cd: audiophile APL 101.523/audite 21.423

david diamond rounds for string orchestra; piston symphony no 2
cd: audite 21.423

404/20 may 1950/telefunken sessions in berlin jesus-christus-kirche
paul hindemith
philharmonisches konzert

35951	SK 3795
35952	
35953	SK 3796
35954	
35955	SK 3797
35956	

lp: LE 6567/capitol P 8134

405/11 june 1950/rehearsal recording in bremen grosser glockensaal
wilhelm furtwängler
beethoven leonore no 2 overture
lp: french furtwängler society SWF 8602/japan GMV 108/AT 07-08
cd: refrain DR 92 0031/french furtwängler society SWF 921-922
this brief extract is dimly recorded

406/18 june 1950/sender freies berlin recording without audience in titania palast
wilhelm furtwängler
schubert symphony no 9 in d944 "great"
lp: japan AT 05-06
cd: refrain DR 92 0023

407/20 june 1950/rias berlin recordings in titania palast
wilhelm furtwängler
handel concerto grosso in d minor op 6 no 10
lp: deutsche grammophon 2535 806/japan P 1001
cd: virtuoso 269 7402/audite 21.403

brahms haydn variations op 56a
lp: deutsche grammophon 2535 164/cetra FE 16
cd deutsche grammophon 415 6622/427 4022/474 0302/virtuoso 269 9072/french furtwängler society SWF 062-064/audite 21.403

407/20 june 1950/rias berlin recordings/concluded
hindemith konzert für orchester
lp: cetra FE 22/nippon columbia OZ 7593
cd: cetra CDE 1049/virtuoso 269 7322/music and arts CD 713/
german furtwängler society MMS 9010/audite 41.203

beethoven symphony no 3 in e flat op 55 "eroica"
lp: victor (japan) RCL 3334
cd: german furtwängler society MMS 9010/
music and arts CD 711/audite 21.403

408/22 june-4 july 1950/dg sessions in berlin
jesus-christus-kirche
ferenc fricsay
mendelssohn ein sommernachtstraum: overture, scherzo, ye spotted snakes, intermezzo, nocturne, wedding march, dance of the clowns and finale
with rias-kammerchor/rita streich, soprano/diana eustrati, contralto

01900	LVM 72013
01901	
01902	LVM 72 014
01903	
01904	LVM 72 015
01905	
01906	LVM 72 016
01907	

lp: LPM 18 001/2535 736/2548 201/478 032/heliodor 89 629
cd: 449 3282/479 3578/479 5516

408/june-july 1950/dg sessions in berlin/concluded
johann and josef strauss pizzicato polka
01944   L 62 870
45: NL 32 123
cd: 479 3578
matrix number 01944 was coupled with matrix number 01960 (see session no 394)

strauss till eulenspiegels lustige streiche
02118   LVM 72 024
02119 45: EPL 30 067
lp: LP 16 006/LPEM 19 111/LPEM 19 078/2535 724/
heliodor 89 803/decca (usa) DL 9529
cd: 445 4032/479 3578

berlioz la damnation de faust: marche hongroise
04331   LVM 72 297
45: EPL 30 005/NL 32 305
lp: LPEM 19 061/2535 738/2548 064
cd: 447 3612/479 3578

409/10-16 august 1950/dg sessions in berlin
jesus-christus-kirche
fritz lehmann
prokofiev peter and the wolf
with mathias wieman, narrator
02005   LM 68 443
02006
02007   LM 68 444
02008
02009   LM 68445
lp: LP 16 038/LPE 17 117
78rpm version was also published with french narration (LM 68 459-16 461); lp versions were also published with english (LPEM 19 187), french (LP 16 098/LPE 17 118) and spanish (LPE 17 119) narrations

haydn symphony no 94 in g "surprise"
02169   LVM 72 039
02170
02171   LVM 72 040
02172
lp: LP 16 012/LPE 17 189/LPM 18 397/478 402/
heliodor 89 799/decca (usa) DL 9617

410/25 september 1950/sender freies berlin recordings in titania palast

bruno walter

beethoven egmont overture
lp: discocorp BWS 726/BWS 1010
cd: music and arts CD 239/arkadia CDGI 738

mozart symphony no 40 in g minor k550
lp: discocorp BWS 726
cd: music and arts CD 239
final movement of the symphony also filmed for newsreel footage; this movement also published in separate lp editions where it was incorrectly attributed to wilhelm furtwängler
vhs video: teldec 4509 950386
laserdisc: teldec 4509 950383
dvd: teldec 0927 426672

brahms symphony no 2 in d op 73
cd: music and arts CD 239/arkadia CDGI 738/urania/legends LGD 148

411/5-6 november 1950/sender freies berlin recordings in titania palast

hans knappertsbusch

beethoven coriolan overture
cd: green hill GH 0006-0007/tahra TAH 417-418/archipel ARPCD 0150

brahms symphony no 3 in f op 90
lp: hans-knappertsbusch-gesellschaft HK 1020
cd: chaconne CHCD 1005/rare moth RM 416/andromeda ANDRCD 5066/istituto discografico italiano IDIS 6362

412/6-8 december 1950/rias berlin recordings without audience in jesus-christus-kirche
sergiu celibidache
carlos chavez ramirez sinfonia de antigona; gunther raphael symphony no 4 in c
cd: audite 21.423

413/7 december 1950/sender freies berlin recording in titania palast
sergiu celibidache
genzmer flute concerto
with gustav scheck, flute
cd: audiophile APL 101.523/audite 21.406

414/8 january 1951/rias berlin recording without audience in jesus-christus-kirche
hans knappertsbusch
bruckner symphony no 8 in c minor
cd: arkadia CDGI 711/music and arts CD 4856/CD 1028/green hill GH 0006-0007/tahra TAH 207-208/documents 222 334/andromeda ANDRCD 9010/audite 41.405

415/9-16 january 1951/dg sessions in berlin
jesus-christus-kirche
ferenc fricsay
rossini la scala di seta overture
02370   LVM 72 061
45: EPL 30 064
lp: LPEM 19 041
cd: 477 5908/479 3578

johann strauss wiener blut waltz
02379   LVM 72 052
45:   EPL 30 073
cd: 479 3578/tahra TAH 454

bartok violin concerto no 2
with tibor varga, violin
02426   LVM 72 075
02427
02428   LVM 72 076
02429
02430   LVM 72 077
02431
lp: LPM 18 006
cd: 445 4002/479 3578

416/20-23 february 1951/philips sessions in berlin
jesus-christus-kirche
fritz lehmann
mozart symphony no 35 in d k385 "haffner"
lp: A00111R/S04008L/SBL 5201/G03008L/695 014KL/
200 044WGY/epic (usa) LC 3006
cd: 442 9128

mozart march in d k249
lp: A00111R/S04008L/SBL 5201
cd: 442 9128

cherubini anacreon overture
             A11159G
lp: A00115R
cd: 442 9128

marcel poot ouverture joyeuse
             A11161G
lp: A00115R
cd: 442 9128

weber euryanthe overture
             A11160G
lp: A00115R/GBL 5556/G03052L
cd: 442 9128

sibelius valse triste
             A11161G
45: SBF 135
lp: A00115R
cd: 442 9128

417/3-11 march 1951/telefunken sessions in berlin lichterfelder festsäle
joseph keilberth
beethoven egmont overture
36341   E 3878/VSK 9025
36342
lp: capitol P 8164

brahms symphony no 1 in c minor op 68
lp: LSK 7008/LGX 66003/capitol P 8153
cd: teldec 8.43193/9031 738602

418/19 march 1951/rias berlin recording in titania palast
eugen jochum
beethoven symphony no 6 in f op 68 "pastoral"
lp: movimento musica 08.001

419/24-25 march 1951/dg sessions in berlin jesus-christus-kirche
eugen jochum
brahms symphony no 2 in d op 73
02746   LVM 72 080
02747
02748   LVM 72 081
02749
02750   LVM 72 082
02751
lp: LPM 18 008/LPM 18 360/LPM 18 451-18 454/478 085/ decca (usa) DL 9556
cd: 449 7152/479 6314

420/31 march 1951/rias berlin recording without audience in berlin-zehlendorf gemeindehaus
sergiu celibidache
milhaud suite francaise
cd: audite 21.423/berliner philharmoniker BPH 0605

421/19-25 april 1951/egyptian radio recordings in cairo and alexandria
wilhelm furtwängler
tchaikovsky symphony no 6 in b minor op 64 "pathetique"
lp: deutsche grammophon 2535 165/longanesi GCL 23
cd: deutsche grammophon 474 0302

wagner parsifal karfreitagszauber
lp: deutsche grammophon 2535 826/2721 202/2740 260
cd: deutsche grammophon 415 6632/427 4062/439 8372/ 474 0302/music and arts CD 794/archipel ARPCD 0261

bruckner symphony no 7 in e
lp: deutsche grammophon 2535 161/2721 202/2740 201/2740 260
cd: deutsche grammophon 439 8372/445 4182

422/1 may 1951/rai roma recordings in rome auditorium del foro italico
wilhelm furtwängler
bruckner symphony no 7 in e
lp: rococo 2105/discocorp RR 416/cetra FE 42/nippon columbia OZ 7601
cd: arkadia CDWFE 362/music and arts CD 698/documents 222 128/ tahra FURT 1098/myto 00183

422/1 may 1951/rai roma recordings in rome/concluded
debussy trois nocturnes: nuages et fetes
lp: discocorp BWS 708/DIS 708/cetra FE 15
cd: cetra CDE 1044/music and arts CD 719/myto 00183

strauss don juan
lp: cetra FE 41
cd: myto 00183

wagner tannhäuser overture
lp: discocorp RR 413/deutsche grammophon 2535 826/2740 260
cd: deutsche grammophon 415 6632/427 4062/474 0302/myto 00183/music and arts CD 794/archipel ARPCD 0261

423/22-23 may 1951/dg sessions in berlin
jesus-christus-kirche
eugen jochum
schumann piano concerto in a minor op 54
with monique haas, piano
02717   LVM 72 089
02718
02719   LVM 72 090
02720
lp: LP 16 007/LPE 17 142/heliodor 89 521/decca (usa) DL 7522
cd: 477 6201/479 6314

424/26-30 may 1951/philips sessions in berlin
jesus-christus-kirche
paul van kempen/*eugen jochum
beethoven symphony no 3 in e flat op 55 "eroica"
lp: A00177:/ABL 3013/GBL 5514/G03013L/G03058L/695 001KL/
832 008PGY/epic (usa) LC 3016
cd: 438 5332/442 9128

mendelssohn hebrides overture
45: SBF 169/313 058SF
lp: S06054R
cd: 442 9128/tahra TAH 512-513

*beethoven symphony no 5 in c minor op 67
lp: A00102L/NBR 6050/N00766R/GBL 5556/G05332R/
epic(usa) LC 3002
cd: 442 9128/tahra TAH 238

425/12-13 june 1951/dg sessions in berlin
jesus-christus-kirche
eugen jochum
weber oberon overture
02806   LV 36 002
02807
lp: LPEM 19 037/478 120/decca (usa) DL 4006
cd: 479 6314

wagner lohengrin preludes acts one and three
02947   LV 36 007 (act one)
02948
45: EPL 30 468/NL 32 213
lp: 478 089 (act one)/decca (usa) DL 4030
cd: 477 5484/479 6314

426/18-25 june 1951/philips sessions in berlin
jesus-christus-kirche
willem van otterloo
berlioz symphonie fantastique
lp: A00123L/ABL 3019/A00254L/GBL 5547/G03026L/
epic (usa) LC 3005
cd: 442 9128/retrospective RET 037

427/26-27 june 1951/dg sessions in jesus-christus-kirche
fritz lehmann
handel water music suite
03091   AVM 7401
03092
03093   AVM 7402
03094
03095   AVM 7403
03096
lp: APM 14 006/heliodor 89 766/decca (usa) DL 9594
cd: 457 7582

mendelssohn hebrides overture
03272   LV 36 012
03277
45: EPL 30 445/NL 32 016
lp: LPE 17 044/LPX 29 253/LPX 29 309/478 100/
heliodor 89 673/decca (usa) DL 4015

428/2-6 july 1951/dg sessions in berlin jesus-christus-kirche
paul van kempen
reger variations and fugue on a theme of adam hiller
02727   LVH 72 091
02728
02729   LVH 72 092
02730
02731   LVH 72 092
lp: LPM 18 074
cd: 479 5516

rossini wilhelm tell overture
02810   LVH 72 115
02811
45: EPL 30 099
lp: LPE 17 056
cd: 479 5516

berlioz benvenuto cellini overture
03440   LV 36 023
03441
45: NL 32 037
cd: 479 5516

429/5 september 1951/rias berlin recording in schiller-theater
wilhelm furtwängler
gluck alceste overture
lp: deutsche grammophon 2535 805/cetra FE 50/japan AT 04
cd: deutsche grammophon 477 0062/refrain DR 92 0018/
elaborations ELA 903/audite 21.403
some editions were incorrectly dated 4 september

430/27 september-6 october 1951/dg sessions in jesus-christus-kirche

fritz lehmann

bach violin concerto in e bwv1042
with tibor varga, violin
        AVM 2429
        AVM 2430
lp: APM 14 050

mendelssohn violin concerto in e minor op 64
with tibor varga, violin
02959   LVM 72 125
02960
02961   LVM 72 126
02962
lp: LP 16 015/LPX 29 253/LPX 29 308/478 409

mendelssohn meeresstille glückliche fahrt overture
03305   LVM 72 171
03306
lp: LPE 17 044/LPX 29 253/LPX 29 308/478 100/heliodor 89 673/decca (usa) DL 4015

haydn cello concerto in c
with enrico mainardi, cello
03977   LVM 72 127
03978
03979   LVM 72 128
03980
lp: LP 16 023/LPM 18 222
cd: 479 5516
recording was completed on 30 june 1952

431/13-14 november 1951/dg sessions in berlin
jesus-christus-kirche
leopold ludwig
tchaikovsky piano concerto no 1 in b flat op 23
with shura cherkassky, piano
03072   LVM 72 129
03073
03074   LVM 72 130
03075
03076   LVM 72 131
lp: LPM 18 013/478 447/heliodor 89 517/contour 2870 120/
decca (usa) DL 9605
cd: 456 7452/457 7512/479 5516

liszt les preludes
03189   LVM 72 143
03190
45: EPL 30 057
lp: LPE 17 034/heliodor 89 673/decca)usa) DL 7530
cd: guild GHCD 2381

432/18-19 november 1951/sender freies berlin
recording in titania palast
karl böhm
beethoven violin concerto in d op 61
with christian ferras, violin
lp: victor (japan) RCL 3323
cd: green hill GH 0004

433/22 november-5 december 1951/dg sessions in berlin
jesus-christus-kirche
wilhelm furtwängler
haydn symphony no 88 in g
03138   LVM 72 157
03139
03140   LVM 72 158
03141
lp: LPM 18 015/LPM 18 283/LPM 18 725/LPM 18 858/KL 27-32/
478 146/2535 828/2721 202/2730 005/2740 260/heliodor
88 007/decca (usa) DX 119/DL 9767/heliodor (usa) H 25073
cd: 415 6612/427 4042/439 8392/447 4392/479 5516/
japanese furtwängler centre WFHC 011

furtwängler symphony no 2 in e minor
lp: LPM 18 017-18 018/LPM 18 114-18 115/2707 086/2721 202
cd: 439 8372/457 7222

schubert symphony no 9 in c d944 "great"
03142   LVM 72 153
03143
03144   LVM 72 154
03145
03146   LVM 72 155
03147
03148   LVM 72 156
03149
lp: 18 015-18 016/LPM 18 347/KL 27-32/2535 808/2721 202/
2730 005/2740 260/heliodor 88 006/eterna 820 068/
decca (usa) DX 119/DL 9746/heliodor (usa) H 25074/
HS 25074
cd: 415 6602/427 4052/439 8322/447 4392/479 5516/
naxos 8.111344

434/december 1951/film and sound recordings in berlin titania palast for the film "botschafter der musik"
wilhelm furtwängler
wagner die meistersinger von nürnberg overture: opening bars; schubert symphony no 8 "unfinished": rehearsal of opening section; strauss till eulenspiegels lustige streiche
lp: period SPL 716/everest SDBR 3252 (meistersinger and till)/ nippon columbia OS 7076 (schubert and till)
cd: french furtwängler society SWF 8403-8404 (schubert)
vhs video: teldec 4509 950383/4509 957103 (till)
laserdisc: teldec 4509 950386
dvd: teldec 0927 426672 (meistersinger and schubert)/ 0927 426682 (till)
complete performance of till eulenspiegel film includes a super-imposed ballet sequence

435/17 december 1951/rias berlin recording in berlin titania palast
karl böhm
dvorak symphony no 9 "from the new world"
lp: movimento musica 01.1024

436/26 december 1951/sender freies berlin recording in titania palast
artur rother
beethoven symphony no 1 in c op 21
lp: urania URLP 101
cd: tuxedo TUXCD 1081

437/14-21 january 1952/dg sessions in berlin
jesus-christus-kirche
paul van kempen
brahms piano concerto no 2 in b flat op 83
with adrian aeschbacher, piano
03388   LVM 72 177
03389
03390   LVM 72 178
03391
03392   LVM 72 179
03393
03394   LVM 72 180
03395
lp: LPM 18 024
cd: 479 5516/tahra TAH 512-515

brahms academic festival overture
03442   LV 36 028
03443
45: EPL 30 248
lp: LPE 17 056
cd: 479 5516

438/29 january 1952/rias berlin recordings without audience in jesus-christus-kirche
hans knappertsbusch
johann strauss 1001 nacht intermezzo
cd: curcio CON 17/green hill GHCD 0006-0007/
tahra TAH 214-215/audite 21.405
tahra incorrectly describes this work as boldemann la danza

beethoven symphony no 8 in f op 93
lp: movimento musica 08.001
cd: arkadia CDGI 723/chaconne CHCD 1005/documents 205 229/ 222 334/andromeda ANDRCD 5017/urania URN 22217/tahra TAH 214-215/audite 21.405

439/10 february 1952/sender freies berlin recordings in titania palast
wilhelm furtwängler
beethoven grosse fuge op 133
lp: deutsche grammophon LPM 18 859/2535 813/heliodor 88 023
cd: deutsche grammophon 477 0062/german furtwängler society TMK 2006 01920/pristine audio PASC 370

honegger mouvement symphonique no 3
lp: cetra FE 15
cd: cetra CDE 1044/virtuoso 269 7322/music and arts CD 719/ german furtwängler society TMK 05294/TMK 2006 01920/ french furtwängler society SWF 001-002

439/10 february 1952/sender freies berlin recordings/
concluded
schubert symphony no 8 in b minor d759 "unfinished"
lp: deutsche grammophon 2535 805/2721 202
cd: deutsche grammophon 423 5722/439 8322/474 0302/
virtuoso 269 7322/german furtwängler soiety TMK 2006 01920

brahms symphony no 1 in c minor op 68
lp: deutsche grammophon 2535 162/2721 202
cd: deutsche grammophon 415 6622/415 4022/439 8322/
477 0062/virtuoso 269 9072/japanese furtwängler society
WFJ 25-26/french furtwängler society SWF 062-064/
german furtwängler society TMK 2006 01920

440/2-3 march 1952/rias berlin recording in titania palast
leopold ludwig
bruckner symphony no 3 in d minor
lp: allegro royale 1379
published pseudonymously with the conductor named as gerd ruhban

441/28 march-2 april 1952/dg sessions in berlin
jesus-christus-kirche
eugen jochum
bruckner symphony no 7 in e
lp: LPM 18 112-18 113/LPM 18 033-18 034/decca (usa) DXE 146
cd: 479 6314/tahra TAH 269

442/7 may 1952/bayerischer rundfunk recording in munich deutsches museum
wilhelm furtwängler
brahms symphony no 2 in d op 73
lp: emi 1C147 50336-50339M/1C149 53420-53426M/1C049 01532/
2C153 53420-53426/3C153 53661-53669M
cd: virtuoso 269 9072/emi 252 3212/565 5132/907 8782/french furtwängler society SWF 062-064/pristine audio PASC 341

443/25-26 may 1952/electrola sessions in berlin jesus-christus-kirche
wilhelm furtwängler
mendelssohn violin concerto in e minor op 64
with yehudi menuhin, violin
reel-to-reel tape: HTA 2
45: victor WDM 1720
lp: ALP 1135/FALP 112/GHLP 1016/QALP 10071/electrola E 90074/
WALP 1135/E 60546/WDLP 602/SME 91486/SMVP 8040/victor
LM 1720/emi 1C047 00907/2C051 03612
cd: movimento musica 051 052/emi 747 1192/769 7992/
566 9752/907 8782

444/4-5 june 1952/dg session in berlin jesus-christus-kirche
ferdinand leitner
brahms alto rhapsody
with berliner liedtafel/elisabeth höngen, contralto
03853   LVM 72 231
03854
lp: LP 16 105/LPX 29 256/decca (usa) DL 4074
cd: 457 9732

445/9-15 june 1952/dg sessions in berlin
jesus-christus-kirche

fritz lehmann

bach cantata no 1 "wie schön leuchtet der morgenstern"
with berliner motettenchor/gunthild weber, soprano/
helmut krebs, tenor/hermann schey, bass
        AVM 2937
        AVM 2938
lp: AP 13 018/APM 14 079/decca (usa) DL 9671
cd: 445 0582

bach cantata no 19 "es erhub sich ein streit"
with berliner motettenchor/gunthild weber, soprano/
helmut krebs, tenor/hermann schey, bass
lp: APM 14 005/decca (usa) DL 9671

bach cantata no 21 "ich hatte viel bekümmernis"
with berliner motettenchor/gunthild weber, soprano/
helmut krebs, tenor/hermann schey, bass
lp: APM 14 007/decca (usa) DL 9673

bach cantata no 39 "brich dem hungrigen dein brot"
with berliner motettenchor/gunthild weber, soprano/
lore fischer, contralto/hermann schey, bass
lp: AP 13 003/APM 14 080/decca (usa) DL 9672

bach cantata no 79 "gott der herr ist sonn' und schild"
with berliner motetenchor/gunthild weber, soprano/
lore fischer, contralto/hermann schey, bass
lp: APM 14 005/decca (usa) DL 9672

445/9-15 june 1952/dg sessions in berlin/concluded
bach cantata no 105 "herr gehe nicht ins gericht!"
with berliner motettenchor/gunthild weber, soprano/
lore fischer, contralto/helmut krebs, tenor/
hermann schey, bass
    AVM 2441
    AVM 2442
lp: AP 13 002/APM 14 080/decca (usa) DL 9682

446/18-29 june 1952/dg sessions in berlin
jesus-christus-kirche
fritz lehmann
brahms tragic overture
03803 LVM 72 282
03804
lp: LP 16 024/LPEM 19 154/478 401/decca (usa) DL 4048

mozart die zauberflöte overture; don giovanni overture
03855 LVM 72 237
03856
45: EPL 30 022/decca (usa) ED 3534
lp: LPM 18 091/LPEM 19 040/LPE 17 014 (giovanni)/
478 074/heliodor 89 762/decca (usa) DL 4035
recording of don giovanni overture completed on 9 july 1952

chopin piano concerto no 2 in f minor
with stefan askenase, piano
03970 LVM 72 228
03971
03972 LVM 72 229
03973
03974 LVM 72 230
lp: LP 17 174/LPM 18 040/478 086
cd: 477 5242

447/9-10 july 1952/dg sessions in jesus-christus-kirche
fritz lehmann
mozart die entführung aus dem serail overture;
cosi fan tutte overture
03858   LV 36 050
03859
45: EPL 30 014/NL 32 018 (entführung)
lp: LPM 18 091/LPEM 19 015 (entführung)/LPEM 19 040/
478 014/heliodor 89 762/decca (usa) DL 4035
cd: 477 5812 (cosi)

mozart nozze di figaro overture; der schauspieldirektor overture
03862   L 62 891
03860
45: NL 32 018
lp: LPM 18 091/LPEM 19 040/LPEM 19 066 (figaro)/478 074/
heliodor 89 762/decca (usa) DL 4036

mozart la clemenza di tito overture; idomeneo overture
            LV 36 060
45: EPL 30 479/NL 32 051
lp: LPM 18 091/LPEM 19 040/478 074/heliodor 89 762/
decca (usa) DL 4035 (clemenza)/DL 4036 (idomeneo)
cd: 477 5812

448/4-7 september 1952/dg sessions in berlin jesus-christus-kirche
paul van kempen
brahms hungarian dances nos 1, 3, 5, 6, 17, 18, 19, 20 and 21
04092   LV 36 054
04093
04094   LV 36 055
04095
45: EPL 30 028 (nos 1, 6, 17, 18, 19 and 20)/
NL 32 010 (nos 3 and 5)
lp: LPE 17 068
cd: 479 5516

beethoven die weihe des hauses overture
            LVM 72 470
lp: LP 16 126/LPE 17 063
cd: 438 5332

449/28-29 september 1952/sender freies berlin recording in titania palast
hans knappertsbusch
wolf italian serenade, arranged by max reger
lp: discocorp RR 426
cd: refrain DR 92 009/rare moth RM 416

450/7-10 november 1952/dg sessions in berlin
jesus-christus-kirche
fritz lehmann
weber der freischütz overture
04312   LV 36 070
04313
lp: LPM 18 058/LPEM 19 013/LPEM 19 037/478 120/heliodor 89 537/89 858/decca (usa) DL 4075/DL 9797/DL 9896/ heliodor (usa) H 25016/HS 25016

gluck alceste overture
04360   LV 36 073
04361
45: EPL 30 122
lp: heliodor 89 504/decca (usa) DL 4075

handel music for the royal fireworks
04407   AVM 7410
04408
04409   AVM 7411
04410
lp: AP 13 012/decca (usa) DL 9696
cd: 457 7582

beethoven coriolan overture
05714   LVM 72 455
05715
45: EPL 30 122
lp: LPM 18 234/LPEM 19 037/LPE 17 072/478 139/ decca (usa) DL 4068

451/12-14 november 1952/dg sessions in berlin
jesus-christus-kirche
eugen jochum
beethoven symphony no 7 in a op 92
04320   LVM 72 294
04321
04322   LVM 72 295
04323
04324   LVM 72 296
04325
lp: LPM 18 069/LPEM 19 293-19 299/478 439/
decca (usa) DL 9690
cd: 474 0182/479 6314

452/25-27 november 1952/dg sessions in berlin
jesus-christus-kirche
fritz lehmann
schubert symphony no 8 in b minor d759 "unfinished"
04251   LVM 72 292
04252
04253   LVM 72 293
04254
lp: LPM 18 283/LP 16 051/LPE 17 035/LPX 29 252/478 134/
heliodor 89 625/decca (usa) DL 9696
cd: magdalen METCD 8020

452/25-27 november 1952/dg sessions in berlin/concluded
**schubert rosamunde: alfonso und estrella overture,
entr'acte no 1, ballet music no 1, entr'acte no 2,
romanze, geisterchor, entr'acte no 3, hirtenmelodie,
hirtenchor, jägerchor, ballet music no 2
and die zauberharfe overture**
with berliner motettenchor

04723	LVM 72 369
04724	
04725	LVM 72 370
04726	
04727	LVM 72 371
04728	
04729	LVM 72 372
04730	
04731	LVM 72 373
04732	

lp: LPM 18 101-18 102/LPX 29 334
cd: 474 9862

recording completed on 27 january 1953; although 78rpm variable grade catalogue numbers were allocated, it is not entirely clear if these were actually published

453/7 december 1952/sender freies berlin recordings in titania palast
wilhelm furtwängler
weber der freischütz overture
lp: cetra FE 50
cd: tahra FURT 1026

hindemith die harmonie der welt
this recording remains unpublished

beethoven symphony no 3 in e flat op 55 "eroica"
lp: rococo 2050/discocorp RR 520/german furtwängler society F666.848M/japan WFJ 1/nippon columbia OZ 7584/OW 7818
cd: refrain DR 93 0065/music and arts CD 520/tahra FURT 1018/FURT 1060-1062/chibas restorations 1128

454/8 december 1952/rias berlin recordings in titania palast
wilhelm furtwängler
weber der freischütz overture
lp: german furtwängler society F670.027-028/japan AT 04
cd: music and arts CD 795/tahra FURT 1026/audite 21.403

hindemith die harmonie der welt
lp: discocorp RR 438/german furtwängler society F670.027-028
cd: music and arts CD 713/japanese furtwängler society WFJ 13-14/audite 21.403

beethoven symphony no 3 in e flat op 55 "eroica"
lp: cetra LO 530
cd: rodolphe RPC 32522-32524/RPV 32801/arkadia CDWFE 363/music and arts CD 869/emblem EF 4001/tahra FURT 1008-1009/FURT 1054-1057/FURT 2002-2004/chibas restorations 1130/audite 21.403

455/31 december 1952/fragmentary newsreel film footage at berlin presseball
wilhelm furtwängler
johann strauss kaiserwalzer
vhs video: teldec 4509 957106
dvd: teldec 0927 426682

456/9-15 january 1953/dg sessions in jesus-christus-kirche
ferenc fricsay
smetana ma vlast: the moldau
04390   LVM 72 320
04391
45: EPL 30 049
lp: LPE 17 018/2535 728/478 428/decca (usa) DL 9760
cd: 479 3578

beethoven symphony no 1 in c op 21
lp: LPM 18 100/478 080/2548 143/2730 016/heliodor 89 613/decca (usa) DL 9626
cd: 479 3578/479 5516

457/23-25 january 1953/dg sessions in jesus-christus-kirche
ferdinand leitner
mozart piano concerto no 23 in a k488
with monique haas, piano
04523   LVM 72 349
04524
04525   LVM 72 350
04526
lp: LPM 18 491/LP 16 056
cd: 477 5808/477 6201

458/13-16 february 1953/dg sessions in jesus-christus-kirche
fritz lehmann
beethoven symphony no 2 in d op 36
04621   LVM 72 342
04622
04623   LVM 72 343
04624
04625   LVM 72 344
lp: LPM 18 477/LP 16 059/478 082/heliodor 89 855
cd: magdalen METCD 8020

459/21-25 february 1953/dg sessions in jesus-christus-kirche
igor markevitch
mussorgsky-ravel pictures at an exhibition
04671   LVM 72 370
04672
04673   LVM 72 371
04674
lp: LP 16 061/LPE 17 137/heliodor 89 669/decca (usa) DL 9782
cd: 437 9462/459 0672/477 5479

460/26 february-3 march 1953/dg sessions in berlin
jesus-christus-kirche
leopold ludwig
liszt piano concerto no 1 in e flat
with andor foldes, piano
04615   LVM 72 384
04616
04617   LVM 72 385
lp: LPM 18 133/479 002/heliodor 89 567
cd: 479 5516/guild GHCD 2381

liszt piano concerto no 2 in a
with andor foldes, piano
04618   LVM 72 386
04619
04620   LVM 72 387
lp: LPM 18 133/479 002/heliodor 89 567
cd: 479 5516/guild GHCD 2381

grieg piano concerto in a minor
with adrian aeschbacher, piano
04570   LVM 72 410
04571
04572   LVM 72 411
04573
lp: LP 16 075/LPE 17 143/heliodor 89 521/contour 2870 122

461/23-25 march 1953/dg sessions in jesus-christus-kirche
karl böhm
beethoven symphony no 5 in c minor op 67
04666   LVM 72 346
04667
04668   LVM 72 347
04669
04670   LVM 72 348
lp: LPM 18 097
cd: 474 9842

462/8-9 april 1953/dg sessions in jesus-christus-kirche
ferenc fricsay
beethoven symphony no 8 in f op 93
04745   LVM 72 364
04746
04747   LVM 72 365
04748
lp: LPM 18 100/478 080/2548 143/2730 015/heliodor 89 613/ decca (usa) DL 9626
cd: 479 3578

463/14 april 1953/sender freies berlin recordings in titania palast
wilhelm furtwängler
beethoven symphony no 8 in f op 93
lp: german furtwängler society F666.624-625/discocorp RR 413/
japan WFJ 2-3/cetra FE 48/nippon columbia OZ 7585
cd: rodolphe RPC 32522-32524/music and arts CD 942/
deutsche grammophon 415 6662/427 4012/477 0062/
tahra FURT 2002-2004/japanese furtwängler society WFJ 24/
german furtwängler society TMK 014128/pristine audio PASC 359

strauss till eulenspiegels lustige streiche
lp: german furtwängler society F666.624-625/japan WFJ 2-3
cd: nuova era 013.6317/virtuoso 269 7302/german
furtwängler society TMK 014128

beethoven symphony no 7 in a op 92
lp: german furtwängler society F666.624-625/japan WFJ 2-3/
discocorp RR 476/cetra FE 4
cd: rodolphe RPC 32422-32424/music and arts CD 942/deutsche
grammophon 415 6662/427 4012/474 0302/tahra FURT 2002-2004/
german furtwängler society TMK 014128

464/16 april 1953/rehearsal and rehearsal performance in hamburg musikhalle
wilhelm furtwängler
ravel valses nobles et sentimentales
lp: japan GMV 105
cd: tahra FURT 1014-1015

465/28-29 april 1953/philips sessions in jesus-christus-kirche
paul van kempen
beethoven symphony no 8 in f op 93
lp: A00179L/A00220-00221L/ABL 3030-3031/GBL 5539/GBR 5601/
G03003L/G05303R/epic (usa) LC 3095
cd: 438 5332/442 9128

466/14 may 1953/dg session in jesus-christus-kirche
wilhelm furtwängler
schumann symphony no 4 in d minor op 120
04866   LVM 72 361
04867
04868   LVM 72 362
04869
04870   LVM 72 363
lp: LP 16 063/LPE 17 170/LPM 18 858/KL 27-32/478 146/2535 805/
2721 202/2730 005/2740 260/heliodor 88 008/lomganesi GCL 15/
decca (usa) DL 9767/heliodor (usa) H 25073/HS 25073
cd: 415 6662/427 4042/439 8322/457 7222/arlecchino ARL 151-152/
japanese furtwängler centre WFHC 011/tahra FURT 1099-1100

467/17-22 may 1953/dg sessions in jesus-christus-kirche
paul van kempen
brahms violin concerto in d op 77
with wolfgang schneiderhan, violin
lp: LPM 18 132/heliodor 89 519
cd: 477 5263

467/17-22 may 1953/dg sessions/concluded
beethoven violin concerto in d op 61
with wolfgang schneiderhan, violin
04871   LVM 72 366
04872
04873   LVM 72 367
04874
04875   LVM 72 368
04876
lp: LPM 18 099/eterna 820 005/decca (usa) DL 9784
cd: 477 5263

beethoven piano concerto no 3 in c minor op 37
with wilhelm kempff, piano
05182   LVM 72 423
05183
05184   LVM 72 424
05185
05185   LVM 72 425
05186
lp: LPM 18 130/LPM 18 371-18 374/2548 344
cd: 435 7442/474 0242

beethoven piano concerto no 4 in g op 58
with wilhelm kempff, piano
05365   LVM 72 450
05366
05367   LVM 72 451
05368
05369   LVM 72 452
lp: LP 16 072/LPE 17 084/LPM 18 310/
LPM 18 371-18 374/2548 190
cd: 435 7442/474 0242

468/18 may 1953/sender freies berlin recordings in titania palast
wilhelm furtwängler
stravinsky le baiser de la fee
lp: discocorp RR 708/DIS 708/cetra FE 14/nippon columbia OZ 7592/
german furtwängler society F668.164-165M
cd: cetra CDE 1043/virtuoso 269 7392/music and arts CD 713/
german furtwängler society TMK 014128/tahra FURT 1019/
japanese furtwängler society WFJ 33-34

beethoven violin concerto in d op 61
with wolfgang schneiderhan, violin
lp: deutsche grammophon LPM 18 855/KL 27-32/2535 809/
2730 005/heliodor 88 024
cd: amadeo 431 3432/431 3452/deutsche grammophon 474 7282/
japanese furtwängler society WFJ 33-34/pristine audio PASC 370

brahms symphony no 1 in c minor op 68
lp: discocorp RR 418/everest SDBR 3437/cetra FE 13/
nippon columbia OZ 7820
cd: german furtwängler society TMK 05298/elaborations ELA 902/
tahra FURT 1019/japanese furtwängler society WFJ 33-34

469/23-29 may 1953/dg sessions in jesus-christus-kirche
paul van kempen
beethoven piano concerto no 5 in e flat op 73 "emperor"
with wilhelm kempff, piano
        LVM 72 407
        LVM 72 408
        LVM 72 409
lp: LPM 18 131/LPM 18 371-18 374/2548 160
cd: 435 7442/474 0242

beethoven piano concerto no 1 in c op 15
with wilhelm kempff, piano
lp: LPM 18 129/LPM 18 371-18 374/2548 130
cd: 435 7442/474 0242

beethoven piano concerto no 2 in b flat op 19
with wilhelm kempff, piano
lp: LP 16 071/LPE 17 083/LPM 18 371-18 374/2548 190
cd: 435 7442/474 0242

470/30 may-1 june 1953/philips sessions in berlin jesus-christus-kirche
paul van kempen
beethoven symphony no 7 in a op 92
lp: A00180L/ABL 3017/GBL 5510/G03050L/695 034KL/
700 045WGY/6747 234/epic (usa) LC 3026
cd: 438 5332/442 9128

471/3-5 june 1953/dg sessions in berlin
jesus-christus-kirche
fritz lehmann
mozart piano concerto no 26 in d k537 "coronation"
with carl seemann, piano
05080   LVM 72 426
05081
05082   LVM 72 427
05083
05084   LVM 72 428
lp: LPM 18 143/478 078/heliodor 89 716/decca (usa) DL 9631
cd: 445 4792/474 6112

472/30 june-4 july 1953/dg sessions in berlin
jesus-christus-kirche
ferenc fricsay
smetana ma vlast: from bohemia's woods and fields
04974   LVM 72 383
04975
45: EPL 30 511
lp: LPE 17 018/LPEM 19 186/478 141/2535 729
cd: 479 3578

tchaikovsky symphony no 6 in b minor op 64 "pathetique"
04976   LVM 72 400
04977
04978   LVM 72 401
04979
04980   LVM 72 402
04981
lp: LPM 18 104/2535 734/heliodor 89 568
cd: 445 4002/457 0782/479 3578

473/8 september 1953/rias berlin recording in berlin titania palast
herbert von karajan
beethoven symphony no 3 in e flat op 55 "eroica"
lp: maestri del secolo APE 1205/wg records WG 30003/joker SM 1337
cd: artemis 710 000/710 003/audite 21.414
karajan's first post-war appearance with the orchestra

474/15 september 1953/rias berlin recordings in berlin titania palast
wilhelm furtwängler
schubert rosamunde overture d644
lp: deutsche grammophon 2535 804/cetra FE 11
cd: arkadia CD 525/CDHP 525/virtuoso 269 7362/seutsche grammophon 415 6602/427 4052/477 0062/audite 21.403

schubert symphony no 8 in b minor d759 "unfinished"
lp: paragon DSV 52101/cetra FE 11/victor (japan) RCL 3337
cd: curcio CON 03/music and arts CD 795/tahra FURT 1017/japanese furtwängler society WFJ 24/audite 21.403

schubert symphony no 9 in c d944 "great"
lp: cetra FE 12/german furtwängler society F670.207-208/longanesi GCL 43
cd: arkadia CD 525/CDHP 525/foyer CDS 16005/emblem EF 4002/music and arts CD 795/tahra FURT 1008-1011/FURT 1017/audite 21.403

475/2-4 november 1953/dg sessions in berlin jesus-christus-kirche
ferdinand leitner
schumann symphony no 3 in e flat op 97 "rheinische"
lp: LP 16 084/LPE 17 239/479 025/heliodor 89 626
cd: 479 5516

mendelssohn ruy blas overture
45: EPL 30 129
lp: LPX 29 324/heliodor 89 549
cd: 449 3282/479 5516

476/9 november 1953/rias berlin recordings without audience in berlin-zehlendorf gemeindenaus and *jesus-christus-kirche
sergiu celibidache
mendelssohn symphony no 4 in a op 90 "italian"
lp: lomganesi GCL 10/cetra LO 53/movimento musica 01.031
cd: arkadia CDGI 734/curcio CON 2/arlecchino ARLA 96/ frequenz 041.010/nuova era NE 6348-6349/audite 21.423/ berliner philharmoniker BPH 0605

bizet symphony in c
cd: audite 21.423

*vivaldi violin concerto rv210
with helmut heller, violin
cd: audite 21.423

477/27 november-4 december 1953/dg sessions in jesus-chrisus-kirche

igor markevitch

berlioz symphonie fantastique
lp: LPM 18 167/decca (usa) DL 9783
cd: 459 0672/474 9872

tchaikovsky symphony no 6 in b minor op 74 "pathetique"
lp: LPM 18 193/decca (usa) DL 9811
cd: 474 4002

478/7-17 december 1953/dg sessions in berlin jesus-christus-kirche

eugen jochum

brahms symphony no 4 in e minor op 98
lp: LPM 18 183/LPM 18 451-18 454/478 079/2548 110/
longanesi GCL 37/memories HR 4246
cd: 449 7152/479 6314

brahms symphony no 1 in c minor op 68
lp: LPM 18 182/LPM 18 541-18 454
cd: 449 7152/479 6314

strauss der rosenkavalier: act three walzerfolge
45: EPL 30 056
lp: LPE 17 020/LPEM 19 015
cd: 479 6314

479/6-10 january 1954/dg sessions in jesus-christus-kirche
fritz lehmann
strauss don juan
lp: LP 16 091/LPEM 19 154/478 401

debussy prelude a l'apres-midi d'un faune
45: EPL 30 311
lp: LP 16 091/LPEM 19 154/478 401/heliodor 89 815

480/1-9 february 1954/dg sessions in jesus-christus-kirche
eugen jochum
beethoven symphony no 3 in e flat op 55 "eroica"
lp: LPM 18 179/LPEM 19 293-19 299/478 072/
heliodor 89 642/decca (usa) DL 9865
cd: 474 0182/479 6314

strauss schlagoberswalzer
05531   LVM 72 474
05532
45: EPL 30 056
lp: LPE 17 020
cd: 479 6314

481/10-13 february 1954/dg sessions in jesus=christus-kirche
fritz lehmann
de falla el sombrero de 3 picos suite
lp: LPM 18 177/LPEM 19 044/heliodor 89 815/decca (usa) DL 9775
cd: 477 5486

mozart piano concerto no 17 in g k453
with andor foldes, piano
lp: LPM 18 457/LP 16 093/LPE 17 184/478 417/
heliodor 89 695/contour 2870 125

482/14 february 1954/dg session in jesus-christus-kirche
leopold ludwig
rachmaninov piano concerto no 2 in c minor
with andor foldes, piano
lp: LPM 18 190/heliodor 89 564
cd: 479 5516
recording completed on 25 april 1954

483/18-28 february 1954/dg sessions in jesus-christus-kirche
igor markevitch
mozart mass in c k317 "coronation"
with hedwigschor/maria stader, soprano/sieglinde wagner, contralto/ helmut krebs, tenor/josef greindl, bass
lp: LP 16 096/LPE 17 141/LPX 29 330/decca (usa) DL 9805
cd: 437 3832

mozart symphony no 34 in c k338
lp: LPM 18 176/478 138/heliodor 89 515/decca (usa) DL 9810
cd: 474 4002/479 5516

mozart symphony no 38 in d k504 "prague"
lp: LPM 18 176/478 138/heliodor 89 515/decca (usa) DL 9805
cd: 474 4002/479 5516

schubert symphony no 3 in d d200
lp: LPM 18 221/478 420/2548 021/decca (usa) DL 9810
cd: 474 4002/474 9852

484/7-10 march 1954/dg sessions in jesus-christus-kirche
fritz lehmann
chabrier espana
04696   LVM 72 352
45: EPL 30 004
lp: LPEM 19 044/decca (usa) DL 9775
cd: 477 5486

de falla el amor brujo
with diana eustrati, contralto
lp: LPE 17 272/LPM 18 177/LPEM 19 044/heliodor 89 815/
decca (usa) DL 9775
cd: 477 5486

485/20-24 march 1954/dg sessions in jesus-christus-kirche
paul hindemith
hindemith die harmonie der welt
lp: LPM 18 181

hindemith sinfonische tänze
lp: LP 16 094/LPM 18 507

486/4-5 april 1954/electrola sessions in berlin musikhochschule
wilhelm furtwängler
beethoven leonore no 2 overture
lp: E 90132/E 70362/E 70421/WALP 1324/WBLP 546/WBLP 563/
ALP 1324/unicorn WFS 4/emi 1C047 00843M/1C149 53432-53439M/
2C153 52540-52551/3C153 53800-53805M
cd: 565 5132/907 8782

487/23 april 1954/rias berlin recording in titania palast
karl böhm
beethoven symphony no 4 in b flat op 60
lp: movimento musica 08.001

488/27 april 1954/rias berlin recordings in titania palast
wilhelm furtwängler
handel concerto grosso in d op 6 no 5
lp: deutsche grammophon 2535 806/japan P 1001
cd: virtuoso 269 7392/deutsche grammophon 477 0062/audite 21.403

brahms symphony no 3 in f op 90
lp: deutsche grammophon 2535 163/longanesi GCL 05
cd: deutsche grammophon 423 5722/477 0062/music and arts CD 941/
french furtwängler society SWF 062-064/pristine audio PASC 342/
audite 21.403

blacher concertante musik
lp: cetra FE 26
cd: as-disc AS 370/audite 21.403

wagner tristan prelude and liebestod
lp: cetra FE 25/german furtwängler society F666.164-165M/
discocorp RR 229
cd: deutsche grammophon 415 6632/427 4062/
474 0302/audite 21.403

489/4 may 1954/radiodiffusion francaise recordings in paris theatre de l'opera
wilhelm furtwängler
weber euryanthe overture
lp: deutsche grammophon 2535 805/cetra LO 519/FE 45
cd: french furtwängler society SWF 942-943/deutsche grammophon 477 0062/tahra FURT 1023-1024/japanese furtwängler society WFJ 42-43

brahms haydn variations op 56a
lp: cetra LO 519/FE 45
cd: curcio CON 14/french furtwängler society SWF 942-943/ elaborations ELA 902/tahra FURT 1023-1024/japanese furtwängler society WFJ 42-43

schubert symphony no 8 in b minor d759 "unfinished"
lp: cetra LO 519/FE 45/japan TPR 1159/discocorp RR 394/nippon columbia OZ 7512/OW 7590/OW 7819
cd: elaborations ELA 901/french furtwängler society SWF 942-943/ tahra FURT 1023-1024/japanese furtwängler society WFJ 42-43

beethoven symphony no 5 in c minor op 67
lp: cetra LO 519/FE 45/discocorp RR 522
cd: elaborations ELA 901/french furtwängler society SWF 942-943/ tahra FURT 1023-1024/japanese furtwängler society WFJ 42-43

490/14 may 1954/rai torino recordings in torino sala del conservatorio

wilhelm furtwängler

weber euryanthe overture
lp: discocorp RR 413/rococo 2106/paragon DSV 52101/cetra FE 50/nippon columbia OZ 7590
cd: as-disc AS 373/tahra FURT 1041-1042

brahms symphony no 3 in f op 90
lp: discocorp RR 418/paragon DSV 52101/nippon columbia OW 7822
cd: nuova era NE 013.6332-6334/tahra FURT 1041-1042

strauss till eulenspiegels lustige streiche
lp: japan AT 13-14
cd: tahra FURT 1042-1043

wagner tristan prelude and liebestod
lp: japan AT 09-10
cd: refrain DR 92 0031/tahra FURT 1042-1043

491/15 may 1954/schweizerische radio- und fernsehgesellschaft recordings in lugano teatro apollo
wilhelm furtwängler
beethoven symphony no 6 in f op 68 "pastoral"
lp: cetra LO 529/discocorp RR 477
cd: ermitage ERM 120

mozart piano concerto no 20 in d minor k466
with yvonne lefebure, piano
lp: french furtwängler society XPMX 2273/unicorn WFS 11/
cetra LO 529/FE 18/discocorp RR 395
cd: virtuoso 269 7352/cetra CDE 1015/CDE 3009/as-disc
AS 372/ermitage ERM 120/emi 569 4732/
warner (japan) WPCS 12910

strauss till eulenspiegels lustige streiche
lp: cetra LO 529/FE 41
cd: refrain DR 92 0031/tahra FURT 1008-1011

492/23 may 1954/rias berlin recordings in titania palast
wilhelm furtwängler
beethoven symphony no 6 in f op 68 "pastoral"
lp: german furtwängler society F669.310-311/
japan TPR 1159/GHE 86125
cd: arkadia CD 504/CDHP 504/nuova era 013.6300/013.6303/
virtuoso 269 7162/emblem EF 4004/music and arts CD 869/
tahra FURT 1008-1009/FURT 1054-1057/audite 21.403/
chibas restorations 1127

beethoven symphony no 5 in c minor op 67
lp: german furtwängler society F669.310-311
cd: nuovo era 013.6300/013.6305/virtuoso 269 7192/emblem
EF 4003/music and arts CD 869/tahra FURT 1008-1009/
FURT 1032-1033/audite 21.403/chibas restorations 1127

493/25-26 may 1954/dg sessions in jesus-christus-kirche
fritz lehmann
beethoven leonore no 3 overture
05714   LVM 72 455
05715
45: EPL 30 066
lp: LPE 17 072/LPE 17 077/LPM 18 234/LPM 18 477/
478 082/478 139
cd: magdalen METCD 8020

haydn symphony no 45 in f sharp minor "farewell"
lp: LPM 18 194/LPM 18 397/478 402

494/19 september 1954/sender freies berlin recording without audience in titania palast
wilhelm furtwängler
beethoven symphony no 1 in c op 21
lp: movimento musica 08.001/victor (japan) RCL 3333
cd: cetra CDE 1013/rodolphe RPC 32522-32524/music and arts CD 792/ tahra FURT 1025/german furtwängler society TMK 017198

495/3-6 november 1954/dg sessions in jesus-christus-kirche
hans rosbaud
sibelius festivo; the swan of tuonela; finlandia; valse triste
45: EPL 30 097 (valse triste only)
lp: LPE 17 025/LPEM 19 185
cd: 447 4532/477 0892

496/9-19 november 1954/dg sessions in jesus-christus-kirche
eugen jochum
beethoven symphony no 6 in f op 68 "pastoral"
lp: LPM 18 202/LPEM 19 293-19 299/478 429/
heliodor 89 503/decca (usa) DL 9892
cd: 474 0182/479 6314

beethoven symphony no 4 in b flat op 60
lp: LPM 18 206/LPEM 19 293-19 299/478 444
cd: 474 0182/479 5516/479 6314

497/15 november 1954/rias berlin recording without audience in musikhochschule
eugen jochum
brahms piano concerto no 1 in d minor op 15
with solomon, piano
cd: myto MCD 89005

INDEX OF CONDUCTORS

numbers are session (not page) numbers

hermann abendroth 1885-1956
009 013 244 266 302
347 349 354

kurt atterberg 1887-1974
048

thomas beecham 1879-1961
241

hans von benda 1888-1972
236 247 261 268

rafaele benedito 1885-1963
022

john bitter 1909
359 377

leo blech 1871-1958
005 007 012 020 021
036 110 113 114

karl böhm 1894-1981
218 220 328 432 435
461 487

index of conductors/continued

leo borchard 1899-1945

168	170	183	187	190
201	218	230		

hans bund 1898-1982

165	172	174	179

sergiu celibidache 1912-1996

360	361	362	363	364
365	366	367	368	369
372	379	380	381	387
390	392	393	397	401
402	403	412	413	420
476				

emil cooper 1877-1960

010

walther davisson 1885-1973

254

franco ferrara 1911-1985

291

index of conductors/continued

max fiedler 1859-1939

093	277

ferenc fricsay 1914-1963

394	408	415	456	462
472				

oskar fried 1871-1941

034	047

wilhelm furtwängler 1886-1954

027	057	060	065	072
078	112	117	134	136
138	139	147	167	169
210	227	233	240	248
257	267	271	276	279
290	294	307	308	309
310	312	313	314	320
321	322	323	327	331
332	333	335	337	338
339	340	342	348	353
358	370	371	373	374
375	376	384	385	386
388	389	391	395	396
405	406	407	421	422
429	433	434	439	442
443	453	454	455	463
464	466	468	474	486
488	489	490	491	492
494				

index of conductors/continued

george georgescu 1887-1964
280

walther gmeindl 1890-1958
282

paul graener 1872-1944
143

wilhelm grosz
062   071   085   088   090
099

arthur grüber 1910
300

manfred gurlitt 1890-1972
053

gustav havemann 1882-1960
149

robert heger 1886-1976
345

alfred hertz 1872-1942
001

camillo hildebrand 1876-1953
003

index of conductors/continued

paul hindemith 1895-1963

181	404	485

georg hoeberg 1872-1950

287

paul hörbiger 1894-1981

122

jascha horenstein 1898-1973

042	056	059

eugen jochum 1902-1987

154	192	235	239	262
270	301	325	334	336
350	357	378	418	419
423	424	425	431	451
478	480	496	497	

friedrich jung 1897-1975

195	203

herbert von karajan 1908-1989

278	285	298	319	473

joseph keilberth 1908-1968

301	417

index of conductors/continued

paul van kempen 1893-1955

157	246	297	424	428
437	448	465	467	469
470				

koichi kishi 1909-1937

205

alexander kitschin

035   043

bruno kittel 1870-1948

030	037	304	317

erich kleiber 1890-1956

033	038	074	079	082
095	102	126	135	146
152	155	178		

paul kletzki 1900-1973

120	125	131

index of conductors/continued

hans knappertsbusch 1888-1965

032	293	305	311	318
326	329	330	341	343
344	346	356	398	399
400	411	414	438	449

hidemaro konoye 1898-1973

| 229 | 260 |

julius köpsch 1887-1970

055

clemens krauss 1893-1954

315

peter kreuder 1905-1981

236

eduard künneke 1885-1953

249

ernst kunwald 1868-1960

| 028 | 039 |

felix lederer 1877-1957

050

index of conductors/continued

fritz lehmann 1904-1956

295	351	409	416	427
430	445	446	447	450
452	458	471	479	481
484	493			

ferdinand leitner 1912-1996

| 444 | 457 | 475 |

leopold ludwig 1909-1979

| 259 | 296 | 382 | 383 | 431 |
| 440 | 460 | 482 | | |

walter lutze 1891-1980

265

theo mackeben 1897-1953

| 069 | 073 | 077 | 098 |

otto marienhagen

| 015 | 025 | 031 |

igor markevitch 1912-1983

| 459 | 477 | 483 |

index of conductors/continued

alois melichar 1896-1976

066	094	103	105	108
142	144	188	193	202
207	211	214	231	256
273	284			

willem mengelberg 1871-1951

286

selmar meyrowitz 1875-1941

064	067	069	071	075
077	080	083	087	089
091	096	097	100	101
110	116	119	120	121
123	131	133		

joseph müller

160

artur nikisch 1855-1922

002   006

erich orthmann

090   127   153   156

willem van otterloo 1907-1978

426

index of conductors/continued

hans pfitzner 1869-1949

| 014 | 023 | 026 | 041 | 058 |
| 106 | 158 | 289 | | |

julius prüwer 1874-1943

| 029 | 044 | 049 | 054 | 137 |

peter raabe 1872-1945

194

emil reesen 1887-1964

287

wilhelm franz reuss 1886-1945

151	159	160	162	163
164	166	171	172	173
176	177	180		

hans rosbaud 1895-1962

495

max roth 1878

046

index of conductors/continued

artur rother 1885-1972

216	282	355	382	436

victor de sabata 1892-1967

275

max von schillings 1868-1933

004	008	016	140	141

hans schlager

091	109	111	115	118
122	124	128	129	132

clemens schmalstich 1880-1960

104

franz alfred schmidt 1874-1939

148	149	150

hans schmidt-isserstedt 1900-1973

184	189	196	197	199
200	201	206	208	209
212	213	215	217	219
221	223	225	226	232
234	237	243	244a	255
258	264	269	270	281
292				

index of conductors/continued

ernst schrader 1907-1986
354a

franz schreker 1878-1934
018   040   051   094   107

kurt schröder 1888-1962
197

rolf schröder
252

heinz schubert 1908-1945
288

johannes schüler 1894-1966
274   299

norbert schultze 1911-2002
230

rudolf schulz-dornburg 1891-1949
175

index of conductors/continued

georg alfred schumann 1866-1952

161	306

carl schuricht 1880-1967

061	068	084	186	191
204	242	253	304	316

bruno seidler-winkler 1880-1960

019	024	251

richard strauss 1864-1949

052	169	224

igor stravinsky 1882-1971

250

hans unger 1895-1965

145

ernst viebig 1897-1959

075	076	081

bruno walter 1876-1962

011	070	092	410

index of conductors/concluded

hans weisbach 1885-1961
263
frieder weissmann 1898-1984
130
walter wohllebe
017
carl woitschach 1864-1939
124   180   185
albert wolff 1884-1970
045
fritz zaun 1893-1966
352
alexander von zemlinsky 1871-1942
075
fritz zweig 1893-1984
063   073

INDEX OF COMPOSERS AND THEIR WORKS

numbers are session (not page) numbers
*indicates that only sections of a work were recorded

franz abt 1819-1895
gute nacht
128
paul abraham 1892-1960
fantasy on viktoria und ihr husar
081
adolphe adam 1803-1856
si j'etais roi overture
115
isaac albeniz 1860-1909
suite espanola
*022   *075
cantos de espana
*022
eugen d'albert 1864-1932
tiefland-potpourri
129
tiefland-querschnitt
213
kurt atterberg 1887-1974
symphony no 6
048

index of composers and their works/continued

daniel auber 1782-1871

la muette de portici overture
264

fra diavolo overture
007 097

johann sebastian bach 1685-1750

brandenburg concerto no 1
142

brandenburg concerto no 2
105

brandenburg concerto no 3
065

brandenburg concerto no 4
142

brandenburg concerto no 5
188

brandenburg concerto no 6
142

orchestral suite no 3
*057 *206 384 385

chorale preludes arranged by schoenberg
056

prelude and fugue arranged by schoenberg
074

toccata and fugue arranged by melichar
273

index of composers and their works/continued

johann sebastian bach/concluded

italian concerto
225

keyboard concerto bwv1065
145

violin concerto bwv 1042
*120   430

matthäus-passion
*037   317

cantata no 1
445

cantata no 19
445

cantata no 21
445

cantata no 39
445

cantata no 50
186

cantata no 79
445

cantata no 104
*186

cantata no 105
445

index of composers and their works/continued

samuel barber 1910-1981

capricorn concerto

403

bela bartok 1881-1945

violin concerto no 2

415

ludwig van beethoven 1770-1827

symphony no 1

| *009 | 436 | 456 | 494 |

symphony no 2

458

symphony no 3

058	235	303	326	*356
407	424	453	454	473
480	496			

symphony no 4

| 331 | 332 | 487 |

symphony no 5

002	027	*192	240	244
275	333	*344	357	370
371	424	461	489	492

symphony no 6

| 014 | 316 | 342 | 370 | 418 |
| 491 | 492 | 496 | | |

index of composers and their works/continued
ludwig van beethoven/continued

symphony no 7
*014	028	242	262	335
451	463	470		

symphony no 8
*014	*126	*139	158	297
438	462	463	465	

symphony no 9
*078	*117	233	312	314
*330				

missa solemnis
030

piano concerto no 1
469

piano concerto no 2
469

piano concerto no 3
216	467

piano concerto no 4
335	467

piano concerto no 5
194	349	469

violin concerto
053	223	254	339	375
382	432	467	468	

index of composers and their works/continued
ludwig van beethoven/concluded

violin romance no 1
274

violin romance no 2
120   274

grosse fuge
290   439

coriolan overture
011   021   039   082   333
411   450

egmont overture
003   029   102   167   169
262   371   297   410   417

fidelio overture
055   266

leonore no 2 overture
395   *405   486

leonore no 3 overture
028   212   239   366   493

die weihe des hauses overture
448

arrangements from beethoven piano sonatas
100   258

index of composers and their works/continued

hector berlioz 1803-1869

symphonie fantastique

*095   426   477

beatrice et benedict overture

055

benvenuto cellini overture

049   079

le carnaval romain overture

006   011   036   369   377

le corsaire overture

372

danse des sylphes from la damnation de faust

016

marche hongroise from la damnation de faust

016   036   049   065   079   408

georges bizet 1838-1875

l'arlesienne incidental music

*005   *040   *051   *061   *204   *281

carmen-querschnitt

124

carmen-potpourri

101

carmen prelude, entr'actes and arias

011   045   050   064   110

symphony in c

476

index of composers and their works/continued

boris blacher 1903-1975
concertante musik
274   488

alfred blumen 1897
heiteres spiel für orchester
144

luigi boccherini 1743-1805
cello concerto in b flat
268
canzonetta
077
menuetto
003   077   183   295

carl bohm 1844-1920
hast du mich lieb?
128
still wie die nacht
127

francois boieldieu 1775-1834
le caliphe de bagdad overture
214
la dame blanche overture
007

index of composers and their works/continued

arrigo boito 1842-1918

son lo spirito che nega from mefistofele

080

alexander borodin 1833-1887

polovtsian dances from prince igor

| 075 | 300 |

march from prince igor

300

gaetono braga 1829-1907

engellied

118

johannes brahms 1833-1897

symphony no 1

| 262 | 307 | *358 | 417 | 468 |
| 478 | | | | |

symphony no 2

| 093 | 343 | *373 | 410 | 419 |
| 442 | | | | |

symphony no 3

| *112 | 311 | 346 | 396 | 411 |
| 439 | 488 | 490 | | |

symphony no 4

| 275 | 338 | 360 | 384 | 385 |
| *386 | 391 | 478 | | |

index of composers and their works/continued

johannes brahms/concluded

piano concerto no 1
497

piano concerto no 2
277   322   338   *345   437

violin concerto
*157   237   467

haydn variations
338   407   489

academic festival overture
049   093   437

tragic overture
446

alto rhapsody
444

selections from the hungarian dances
054   060   064   448

johannes brandt 1780-1837

o maienzeit!
128

benjamin britten 1913-1976

sinfonia da requiem
366

max bruch 1838-1920

violin concerto no 1
*157   301   351   354

index of composers and their works/continued

anton bruckner 1824-1896

symphony no 3

440

symphony no 4

*307   346

symphony no 5

320

symphony no 6

*337

symphony no 7

042   253   294   *313   395
421   422   441

symphony no 8

388   389   414

symphony no 9

348   398   399

ignaz brüll 1846-1907

wo anders from das goldene kreuz

100

ferruccio busoni 1866-1924

violin concerto

390

emanuel chabrier 1841-1894

espana

255   484

carlos chavez 1899-1978

sinfonia de antigona

412

index of composers and their works/continued

luigi cherubini 1780-1842

anacreon overture

387   416

frideryk chopin 1810-1849

piano concerto no 1

044

piano concerto no 2

445

funeral march from the second piano sonata

100

chopin-potpourri

100

domenico cimarosa 1741-1801

il matrimonio segreto overture

113

aaron copland 1900-1990

appalachian spring

403

arcangelo corelli 1653-1713

gigue and badinerie

261

index of composers and their works/continued

peter cornelius 1824-1874
der barbier von bagdad overture
052   113

octave cremieux 1872-1949
quand l'amour meurt (valse)
111

claude debussy 1862-1918
jeux
381
la mer
372
nocturnes
*366
prelude a l'apres-midi d'un faune
*344   479

leo delibes 1826-1891
coppelia
*137   *187
naila valse
234
sylvia
*108   *187

david diamond 1915-2005
rounds for string orchestra
403

index of composers and their works/continued

gaetono donizetti 1797-1848

son anchio la virtu magica from don pasquale
189

la fille du regiment overture
044

nico dostal 1895-1981

grosses wiener-lied-potpourri
122

antonin dvorak 1841-1904

symphony no 7
354a

symphony no 9
285   435

cello concerto
217   360

violin concerto
301

serenade for strings
261

scherzo capriccioso
082

carnival overture
281

wedding dance from holubka
102

selections from the slavonic dances
065   272

index of composers and their works/continued

manuel de falla 1876-1946

el amor brujo

484

el sombrero de 3 picos

*481

la vida breve

*045

gabriel faure 1845-1924

pelleas et melisande suite

045

friedrich von flotow 1812-1883

alessandro stradella overture

044   089

jungfrau maria from alessandro stradella

128

ach so fromm from marha

128   133

wofgang fortner 1907-1987

violin concerto

396

jean francaix 1912-1997

piano concertino

230

index of composers and their works/continued

friedrich der grosse 1712-1786

fredericiana

127

julius fucik 1872-1918

einzug der gladiatoren

185

wilhelm furtwängler 1886-1954

symphony no 2

*380   433

symphonic piano concerto

271   *276

niels gade 1817-1890

a folk tale

*287

louis ganne 1882-1923

liebe himmlische macht

116   120

hans gansser 1884-1959

deutschland erwache!

150

index of composers and their works/continued

tommaso giordani 1730-1806

caro mio ben

127

alexander glazunov 1865-1936

suite from the middle ages

*010

stenka rasin

043   359a

reinhold gliere 1876-1958

concerto for coloratura

363

christoph willibald gluck 1714-1787

alceste overture

321   429   450

selection from the ballet suite

225

iphigenie in aulis overture

020   044   052   095   347

orfeo ed euridice

*347

benjamin godard 1849-1895

mazurka

088

scenes poetiques

*012

index of composers and their works/continued

charles gounod 1818-1893

faust

*226 *234

marche funebre d'une marionette

012

paul graener 1872-1944

die flöte von sanssouci suite

143

enrique granados 1867-1916

goyescas intermezzo

022

edvard grieg 1843-1907

piano concerto

345 460

selections from the incidental music to peer gynt

003 005 007 047 107
187 199

holberg suite

*012

in autumn overture

007

herzwunden

255

letzter frühling

243

grieg-potpourri

100 105 243

index of composers and their works/continued

franz grothe 1908-1982

eine russische fantasie
077

georg frideric handel 1685-1759

concerto grosso op 6 no 5
279   341   488

concerto grosso op 6 no 6
347

concerto grosso op 6 no 10
340   407

movements from organ concerti
259

concerto for double wind
238

music for the royal fireworks
*238   450

water music
427

hallelujah chorus from messiah
030

dank sei dir herr
096

v'adoro pupille from giulio cesare
096   347

alcina ballet music
126

index of composers and their works/continued

josef haydn 1732-1809

symphony no 45
493
symphony no 88
*183   433
symphony no 91
260
symphony no 92
283
symphony no 94
059   272   305   400   409
symphony no 103
296
symphony no 104
365   401
cello concerto in c
430
cello concerto in d
292
3 deutsche tänze
126
arrangements of string quartet movements (including deutschlandlied)
127   200   295

index of composers and their works/continued

joseph helmesberger 1828-1893
ballsirenen-walzer
171

louis herold 1791-1833
zampa overture
096

richard heuberger 1850-1014
der opernball overture
126

paul hindemith 1895-1962
konzert für orchester
407
philharmonisches konzert
404
konzertmusik
072
piano concerto
392
die harmonie der welt
453   454   485
mathis der maler symphony
181
sinfonische tämze
485
sinfonische metamorphosen über themen von weber
374

index of composers and their works/continued

karl hoeller 1907-1972
cello concerto no 2
395

arthur honegger 1892-1955
symphony no 3
439

engelbert humperdinck 1854-1921
hänsel-und-gretel-querschnitt
166
hänsel-und-gretel-fantasy
047
verdorben ach gestorben from königskinder
173

mikhail ippolitov-ivanov 1959-1935
caucasian sketches
*108   172

ivan ivanovivi 1845-1902
donauwellen-walzer
109   211

armin jaernefelt 1869-1958
berceuse
258

leos janacek 1854-1928
lachian dance no 1
082

index of composers and their works/continued

sidney jones 1861-1946
the geisha-querschnitt
132

emmerich kalman 1882-1953
die czardasfürstin-querschnitt
184
zwei märchenaugen from die zirkusprinzessin
174
tanzen möcht ich walzer
118
fortissimo
085

albert ketelby 1875-1959
in a persian market
122

wilhelm kienzl 1861-1941
selig sind die von verfolgung leiden from der evangelimann
083

yrjö kilpinen 1892-1959
folksong from kukon kuullessa
258

koichi kishi 1909-1939
japan suite
205
sketches of japan
205

index of composers and their works/continued

zoltan kodaly 1882-1967
dances of galanta
275

karl komzak 1850-1905
badner madln walzer
305   400

friedrich kuhlau 1786-1832
elves hill overture
287

eduard künnecke 1885-1953
tänzerische suite
249
glückliche reise overture
249

edouard lalo 1823-1892
le roi d'ys overture
045

peter lange-müller 1850-1926
movements from once upon a time
287
renaissance overture
287

index of composers and their works/continued

josef lanner 1801-1843

hofballtänze
099

pestherwalzer
105

schönbrunnerwalzer
102

blas laserna 1751-1816

tornadilla
200

eduard lassen 1830-1904

allerseelen
129

franz lehar 1870-1948

evawalzer
118

gold und silber walzer
234

die lustige witwe querschnitt
213

schön ist die welt potpourri
091

wolgalied from der zarewitsch
174

rendezvous bei franz lehar
197

index of composers and their works/continued

ruggiero leoncavallo 1867-1919

pagliacci intermezzo
110
pagliacci-fantasy
104

ernst levi 1895-1961

ich kam vom walde hernieder
128

anatol liadov 1855-1941

the enchanted lake
281
kikimora
010
nänie
010
scherzo (totentanz)
010

paul lincke 1866-1948

glühwürmchen-idyll
234
schlösser die im monde liegen from frau luna
222
es war einmal from im reich der indra
222

index of composers and their works/continued

franz liszt 1811-1886

piano concerto no 1
044 460

piano concerto no 2
269 460

hungarian fantasy
263

hungarian rhapsody no 1
006 226

hungarian rhapsody no 2
028 165 266

hungarian rhapsody no 6
234

mazeppa
047

les preludes
047 246 293 311 *356
431

tasso
352

tarantella (venezia e napoli)
126

liebestraum in e flat
090

o lieb so lang du lieben kannst
116 120

komponisten-bildnis franz liszt
215

index of composers and their works/continued

albert lortzing 1801-1851

der waffenschmied overture
044   284

fünftausend taler from der wildschütz
067

zar und zimmermann overture
232

holzschuhtanz from zar und zimmermann
226

lebwohl mein flandrisch mädchen from zar und zimmermann
083

o sancta justitia from zar und zimmermann
067

lortzing-potpourri
087

alexandre luigini 1850-1906

ballet egyptien
108

hans christian lumbye 1810-1874

dream pictures
287

index of composers and their works/continued

martin luther 1483-1548

ein feste burg arranged by georg schumann

161

mit fried und freud fahr ich dahin arranged by georg schumann

161

heinrich marschner 1795-1861

an jenem tag from hans heiling

173

joseph marx 1882-1964

marienlied

229

pietro mascagni 1863-1945

cavalleria rusticana intermezzo

110

no no turiddu from cavalleria rusticana

199

voi lo sapete from cavalleria rusticana

200

cavalleria rusticana potpourri

104

index of composers and their works/continued

jules massenet 1842-1912

ah fuyez douce image from manon
148

phaedre overture
243

scenes pittoresques
012   108

alois melichar 1896-1976

baron neuhaus suite
207

wiener impressionen
273

felix mendelssohn-bartholdy   1809-1847

symphony no 4
475

violin concerto
206   379   430   443

hebrides overture
011   041   044   055   114
424   427

meeresstille glückliche fahrt overture
015   430

ruy blas overture
003   475

index of composers and their works/continued

felix mendelssohn-bartholdy/concluded

selections from the incidental music to ein sommernachtstraum

020   038   057   110   375
377   408

frühlingslied

098

3 fantasies arranged by andreae

183

giacomo meyerbeer 1791-1864

o paradis from l'africaine

148

re dell' onde profonde from l'africaine

080

fackeltanz no 1

054

das feldlager in schlesien overture

135

les huguenots overture

044   063

coronation march from le prophete

049   110

index of composers and their works/continued

darius milhaud 1892-1974

suite francaise

420

movements from suite symphonique

393

wolfgang amadeus mozart 1756-1791

symphony no 32

238

symphony no 33

336 378

symphony no 34

316 483

symphony no 35

416

symphony no 38

483

symphony no 39

*073 296 340 348 351

symphony no 40

391 410

symphony no 41

301

violin concerto no 3

*125 347 402

index of composers and their works/continued
wolfgang amadeus mozart/continued
piano concerto no 17
481
piano concerto no 20
175   491
piano concerto no 23
457
piano concerto no 26
471
clarinet concerto
329
sinfonia concertante for violin and viola
*136
sinfonia concertante for 4 wind
228
adagio for violin and orchestra
223
eine kleine nachtmusik
071   178   227   295
march in d
046
deutsche tänze
038   087
coronation mass
283
requiem
304

index of composers and their works/continued

wolfgang amadeus mozart/continued

la clemenza di tito overture

059 447

cosi fan tutte overture

255 447

don giovanni overture

281 445

die entführung aus dem serail overture

167 255 447

le nozze di figaro overture

059 167 215 325 447

non piu andrai from le nozze di figaro

087

porgi amor from le nozze di figaro

251

dove sono from le nozze di figaro

251

idomeneo overture

038 447

der schauspieldirektor overture

087 447

die zauberflöte

241

die zauberflöte overture

255 445

index of composers and their works/continued

wolfgang amadeus mozart/concluded

marsch der priester from die zauberflöte

113

turkish march

115   226

mozart-potpourri

091

moritz moszowski 1854-1925

spanish dances

097

modest mussorgsky 1839-1881

night on bare mountain

010   260

pictures from an exhibition

459

viktor nessler 1841-1890

behüt dich gott from der trompeter von säckingen

100

otto nicolai 1810-1849

die lustigen weiber von windsor overture

020   182   220   293   400

carl nielsen 1865-1931

overture and dance of the cockerels from maskerade

287

index of composers and their works/continued

vileslav novak 1870-1949

charakterstück aus heinzelmännchens wachparade
129

jacques offenbach 1819-1890

hoffmanns-erzählungen-querschnitt
133

orfee aux enfers overture
061   103   123   214

offenbach-potpourri
098

jan paderewski 1860-1941

minuet in g
098

ernst pepping 1901-1981

symphony no 2
335

hans pfitzner 1869-1949

symphony in c
289

das christelflein overture
014

liebesmelodie from das herz
106

index of composers and their works/continued

hans pfitzner/concluded

overture and act 2 finale from das fest auf solhaugen
014

epilogue and march from das käthchen von heilbronn
014

palestrina three preludes
*318   391

trauermarsch from die rose vom liebesgarten
014

walter piston 1894-1976
symphony no 2
403

amilcare ponchielli 1834-1886
dance of the hours from la gioconda
121

marcel poot 1901-1988
ouverture joyeuse
416

david popper 1843-1913
hungarian rhapsody in d
131

francis popy 1874-1928
ballet suite
108
suite orientale
196

index of composers and their works/continued

serge prokofiev 1891-1953

symphony no 1

363   379

peter and the wolf

409

romeo and juliet second suite

364

giacomo puccini 1858-1924

la boheme potpourri

104

la boheme act three prelude

069

che gelida manina from la boheme

064   170

si mi chiamano mini from la boheme

069   121

o mimi tu piu non tormi from la boheme

176

ch' ella mi creda libero from la fanciulla del west

131   159

madama butterfly potpourri

104   159

un bel di from madama butterfly

183

addio fiorito asil from madama butterfly

153

donna non vidi mai from manon lescaut

159

index of composers and their works/continued

giacomo puccini/concluded

tosca potpourri
180   183

te deum & tre sbirri from tosca
080

recondita armonie from tosca
162

non lo sospiri from tosca
183

vissi d'arte from tosca
121

e lucevan le stelle from tosca
162

nessun dorma from turandot
131

puccini-potpourri
087   097   151

sergei rachmaninov 1873-1943

piano concerto no 2
482

prelude in c sharp minor
090

gunther raphael 1903-1960

symphony no 4
412

index of composers and their works/continued

maurice ravel 1875-1937

daphnis et chloe suite no 2

342

pavane pour une finfante defunte

045

valses nobles et sentimentales

464

vladimir rebikov 1866-1920

berceuse

177

max reger 1873-1916

serenade in g

334

hiller variations

428

fugue from mozart variations

134

mariae wiegenlied

229

ottorino respighi 1879-1936

ancient airs and dances suite no 3

261

feste romane

275

emil von reznicek 1860-1945

donna diana overure

007   126

index of composers and their works/continued

nikolai rimsky-korsakov 1844-1908

scheherazade

047

flight of the bumble bee

108

introduction and cortege from le coq d'or

010

hymne au soleil from le coq d'or

071   200

chant hindou from sadko

199

juventino rosas 1868-1894

über den wellen walzer

129

gioachino rossini 1792-1868

il barbiere di siviglia overture

210   219

una voce poco fa from il barbiere di siviglia

189

la gazza ladra overture

065   097

italiana in algeri overture

264   314

la scala di seta overture

264   415

william tell overture

012   140   206   214   428

index of composers and their works/continued

anton rubinstein 1829-1894

valse caprice

088

melodie and elegie

116

arie des vindex from nero

080

toreador et andalouse

003   054

camille saint-saens 1835-1921

danse macabre

003   019   047

la princesse jaune overture

144

mon coeur s'ouvre a ta voix from samson et dalila

361

pablo sarasate 1844-1908

danza espanola

077

alfredo scassola

suite pastorale

077

index of composers and their works/continued

max von schillings 1868-1933

das hexenlied
141

ständchen des arrigo from mona lisa
004

ingwelde act three prelude
004

erntelied from moloch
004

franz schmidt 1874-1939

beethoven variations
350

notre dame intermezzo
272

franz schreker 1878-1934

kleine suite
094

zwischenspiel und nachtgesang from
der schatzgräber
018

franz schubert 1797-1828

symphony no 3
483

symphony no 5
059   247

index of composers and their works/continued
franz schubert/concluded
symphony no 8

007	033	049	198	202
299	*315	*353	385	398
399	*434	439	452	474
489				

symphony no 9

323	406	433	474

rosamunde overture

065	474

selections from the incidental music to rosamunde

008	057	223	452

moment musical no 3 orchestral arrangement
077
deutsche tänze arranged by webern
113
march d818 arranged by liszt
012
das dreimädlerhaus potpourri arranged by berthe
129

heinz schubert 1908-1945
concertante musik
288
hymnisches konzert
323
prelude and toccata
288

index of composers and their works/continued

georg schumann 1866-1952

3 deutsche tänze

306

robert schumann 1810-1856

symphony no 3

*383   475

symphony no 4

014   026   465

piano concerto

310   345

violin concerto

244a   245

cello concerto

320   *337

manfred overture

396

abendlied

208

tokichi setoguchi 1868-1944

gunkan march

214

shikishmakan march

214

dimitri shostakovich 1906-1975

symphony no 7

368

symphony no 9

372

index of composers and their works/continued

jean sibelius 1865-1957

violin concerto
327

en saga
327

festivo
493

finlandia
231   493

valse triste
255   416   493

diamond in the snow
258

the first kiss
209

schilflied
258

the tryst
209

john philip sousa 1854-1932

el capitan march
180

stars and stripes forever march
180

index of composers and their works/continued

bedrich smetana 1824-1884

from bohemia's woods and fields

472

the moldau

076   272   285   456

the bartered bride overture

055   102

furiant from the bartered bride

226

polka from the bartered bride

110

the bartered bride potpourri

069

louis spohr 1784-1859

violin concerto no 8

208

joseph anton steffan 1726-1797

katharina-potpourri

129

rudi stephan 1887-1915

musik für orchester

390

index of composers and their works/continued

johann strauss senior 1804-1849

radetzky march

236

johann strauss 1825-1899

die fledermaus overture

| 009 | 155 | 193 | 218 | 227 |
| 319 | 400 | | | |

die fledermaus querschnitt

160

die fledrmaus potpourri

218

eine nacht in venedig overture

236

der zigeunerbaron overture

| 044 | 155 | 319 |

1001 nacht intermezzo

| 171 | 438 |

1001 nacht walzer

| 126 | 256 |

accelerationen walzer

126

an der schönen blauen donau

| 102 | 211 | 218 | 394 |

annen polka

085

index of composers and their works/continued
johann strauss/continued
bei uns zu haus walzer
019
frühlingsstimmen
049   099
g'schichten aus dem wienerwald
088   256
kaiserwalzer
049   081   102   252   298
455
künstlerleben walzer
285
lagunenwalzer
099
liebesliederwalzer
049   109
morgenblätter
067
o schöner mai walzer
094
persischer marsch
115
rosen aus dem süden
070   081
seid umschlungen walzer
085

index of composers and their works/continued

johann strauss/concluded

tritsch-tratsch polka
218
wein weib und gesang
126
wiener blut walzer
013   415
johann strauss walzer-potpourri
104
johann strauss potpourri
076
streifzug durch die johann strauss operetten
162

josef strauss 1827-1870
dorfschwalben aus österreich
019   081   155   256
sphärenklänge
099   256

johann and josef strauss
pizzicato polka
171   400   408
perpetuum mobile
012   394

index of composers and their works/continued

richard strauss 1864-1949

don juan
308   374   479

festliches präludium
169

metamorphosen
376

olympische hymne
224

selections from schlagobers ballet music
103   193   480

sinfonia domestica
339

till eulenspiegels lustige streiche
065   082   280   337   372
408   434   463   490   491

tod und verklärung
009   275

aber der richtige from arabella
164

und du wirst mein gebieter sein from arabella
164

waltzes from der rosenkavalier
070   095   182   478

schleiertanz from salome
052   070

orchesterlieder
219   265   308

index of composers and their works/continued

igor stravinsky 1882-1971

le baiser de la fee
468

feux d'artifice
126

firebird suite
034

jeu de cartes
250   402

franz von suppe 1819-1895

banditenstreiche overture
183

boccacio overture
243

dichter und bauer overture
243

flotte burschen overture
236

leichte kavallerie overture
146   214

morgen mittag und nacht in wien overture
109

pique dame overture
232

die schöne galathea overture
044   062   232

index of composers and their works/continued

giuseppe tartini 1692-1770

concerto in d

*200

piotr tchaikovsky 1840-1893

symphony no 2

401

symphony no 4

*191

symphony no 5

| *119 | *147 | 286 | 394 |

symphony no 6

| *011 | *119 | 267 | 278 | *344 |
| 421 | 472 | 477 | | |

piano concerto no 1

| 269 | 286 |

violin concerto

| 382 | 431 |

orchestral suite no 3

*191

serenade for strings

| *263 | *359 | 362 |

romeo and juliet

359a

1812 overture

| 035 | 123 |

index of composers and their works/continued

piotr tchaikovsky/concluded

capriccio italien
061   152   379

selections from casse noisette ballet
190   201   400

selections from sleping beauty ballet
201

fantasy on tchaikovsky themes
144

tchaikovsky komponisten-porträt
213

am tchaikovsky-quell, arrangement by ernst urbach
193

carl teike 1864-1922

alte kameraden
185

ambroise thomas 1811-1896

connais-tu le pays from mignon
100   133

mignon-querschnitt
221

raymonda overture
024   054

heinz tiessen 1887-1971

vorspiel zu einem drama
367

index of composers and their works/continued

siegfried translateur 1875-1945

engellied

111

was blumen träumen walzer

111   132

max trapp 1887-1971

violin concerto

328

giuseppe verdi 1813-1901

aida prelude

255   275

grand march from aida

232

ballet music from aida

232   255

celeste aida from aida

156

ciel mio padre from aida

080

o patria mia from aida

121

aida-querschnitt

163

saper vorreste from un ballo in maschera

063

re dell' abisso from un ballo in maschera

100

eri tu from un ballo in maschera

119

index of composers and their works/continued
giuseppe verdi/continued

per me giunto from don-carlo
170

la forza del destino overture
232

solenne in quest' ora from la forza del destino
069   176

patria oppressa from macbeth
177

fuoco di gioia from otello
177

gia nelle notte densa from otello
164

si per ciel from otello
069   163

niun mi tema from otello
156

la donna e mobile from rigoletto
089

questa o quella from rigoletto
089   097

caro nome from rigoletto
196

pleni patrizi from simone boccanegra
119

la traviata act one prelude
201

la traviata act three prelude
201

index of composers and their works/continued

giuseppe verdi/concluded

de miei bollenti spiriti from la traviata
153

la traviata fantasy
073

ah si ben mio from il trovatore
170

il trovatore querschnitt
133   184

i vespri siciliani overture
119   291

verdi-potpourri
096   153

heinrich vitzthum 1848-1917
das hakenkreuz
150

antonio vivaldi 1678-1741
violin concerto rv210
476

largo from a violin concerto
145

pentcho vladigeroff 1899-1978
hungarian rhapsody
046

index of composers and their works/continued

richard wagner 1813-1883

a faust overture

011   347

der fliegende holländer overture

004   032   052   068   212
266

siegfrieds rheinfahrt from götterdämmerung

083   264

siegfrieds trauermarsch from götterdämmerung

112   167   396

starke scheite from götterdämmerung

149

kaisermarsch

003   110

lohengrin prelude

025   052   065   110   425

lohengrin act three prelude

003   016   025   031   154
425

procession to the minster from lohengrin

003

einsam in trüben tagen from lohengrin

121

atmest du nicht die süssen düfte from lohengrin

064

in fernem land from lohengrin

064   120

index of composers and their works/continued
richard wagner/continued
die meistersinger von nürnberg overture
032   097   149   309   396
*434
die meistersinger von nürnberg act three prelude
082   154   220
am stillen herd from die meistersinger von nürnberg
069
morgenlich leuchtend from die meistersinger von nürnberg
069
orchestral version of morgenlich leuchtend
003
wach auf from die meistersinger von nürnberg
171
euch macht ihr's leicht from die meistersinger von nürnberg
171
verachtet mir die meister nicht from die meistersinger
171
tanz der lehrbuben from die meistersinger von nürnberg
032   264
die meistersinger fantasy
081   108
parsifal prelude
001   003   017   257
karfreitagszauber from parsifal
001   003   016   257   421
verwandlungsmusik act one from parsifal
001   032
verwandlungsmusik act three from parsifal
001

index of composers and their works/continued
richard wagner/continued
rienzi overture
005 029 101 130
allmächtiger vater from rienzi
120
nothung neidliches schwert from siegfried
149
schmiede mein hammer from siegfried
149
siegfried idyll
007 326
tannhäuser overture
003 004 087 154
tannhäuser act three prelude
154
venusberg music from tannhäuser
032
entry of the guests from tannhäuser
032 036 191 264
dich teure halle from tannhäuser
121
wohl wusst ich hier from tannhäuser
064
o du mein holder abendstern from tannhäuser
064

index of composers and their works/continued
richard wagner/concluded
tristan und isolde prelude
004   052
tristan und isolde prelude and liebestod
065   248   262   275   322
488   490
einsam wachend from tristan und isolde
120   127
liebestod from tristan und isolde
120
winterstürme wichen dem wonnemond from die walküre
083
siegmund heiss ich from die walküre
083
walkürenritt from die walküre
032   075   264
wotans abschied und feuerzauber from die walküre
168   270
emil waldteufel 1899-1978
espana
109
estudianita
198

index of composers and their works/continued
carl maria von weber 1786-1826
aufforderung zum tanz, arranged by berlioz
003 102 138 318
clarinet concertino
354a
euryanthe overture
008 047 052 416 489
490
der freischütz overture
014 024 027 061 154
210 342 355 450 453
454
der freischütz act three entr'acte
210
hier im irdischen jammertal from der freischütz
089
schweig einmal still from der freischütz
089
der freischutz querschnitt
221
jubel overture
041
oberon overture
041 084 092 282 359a
425

index of composers and their works/concluded

carl maria von weber/concluded

ozean du ungeheuer from oberon
119

preciosa overture
023   135

komponisten-porträt carl maria von weber
197

jaromir weinberger 1896-1967

schwanda der dudelsackpfeiffer potpourri
067

polka from schwanda der dudelsackpfeiffer
076

hugo wolf 1860-1903

italian serenade
449

orchesterlieder
219   361

carl zeller 1842-1898

der vogelhändler querschnitt
172

fantasy on themes from der vogelhändler
073

carl ziehrer 1843-1922

nachtschwärmerwalzer
122

INDEX OF WORKS BY UNIDENTIFIED COMPOSERS
numbers are session (not page) numbers

german national anthem (1938)
260
japanese national anthem (1938)
260
eine folge unserer schönsten lieder
195   203
gott segne unseren führer (kaiserhymne)
165
horst-wessel-lied
music sometimes attributed to peter cornelius
260
ich liebe dich
088
japanischer laternentanz
118
länder und lieder (traditional songs)
119
liebling nach dem tango
090
mahnung
165
moorröschen
118
musik und liebe
160

index of works by unidentified composers/concluded

ob sie wohl kommen mag
129

potpourri aus winkeln und gassen
132

potpourri aus wiener meister-operetten
066

potpourii of themes from old operas
097

potpourri of themes from old operettas
109

rheinländer-potpourri
124

ständchen
111

sternlein und mond
215

vergiss mein nicht
090

der vogel im walde
215

eine walzer-redoute
111

weihnachtslieder
086

Books published by Travis & Emery Music Bookshop:

Anon.: Hymnarium Sarisburiense, cum Rubricis et Notis Musicis.
Anon.: Säcularfeier des Geburtstages von Ludwig van Beethoven
Agricola, Johann Friedrich from Tosi: Anleitung zur Singkunst.
Allen, Percy: The Stage Life of Mrs. Stirling: With ... C19th Theatre
Bach, C.P.E.: edited W. Emery: Nekrolog or Obituary Notice of J.S. Bach.
Bateson, Naomi Judith: Alcock of Salisbury
Bathe, William: A Briefe Introduction to the Skill of Song
Berlioz, Hector: Autobiography of Hector Berlioz, (2 vols.)
Buckley, Robert John: Sir Edward Elgar
Burney, Charles: The Present State of Music in France and Italy
Burney, Charles: The Present State of Music in Germany, The Netherlands ...
Burney, Charles: Account of an Infant Musician
Burney, Charles: An Account of the Musical Performances ... Handel
Burney, Karl: Nachricht von Georg Friedrich Handel's Lebensumstanden.
Burns, Robert: The Caledonian Musical Museum .. Best Scotch Songs. (1810)
Cobbett, W.W.: Cobbett's Cyclopedic Survey of Chamber Music. (2 vols.)
Corrette, Michel: Le Maitre de Clavecin
Cox, John Edmund: Musical Recollections of the Last Half Century. (2 vols.)
Crimp, Bryan: Dear Mr. Rosenthal ... Dear Mr. Gaisberg ...
Crimp, Bryan: Solo: The Biography of Solomon
Crotch, William: Substance of Several Courses of Lectures on Music
d'Indy, Vincent: Beethoven: Biographie Critique
d'Indy, Vincent: Beethoven: A Critical Biography
d'Indy, Vincent: Cesar Franck (in English)
d'Indy, Vincent: César Franck (in French)
Dianna, B.A.: Benjamin Britten's Holy Theatre
Dolge, Alfred: Pianos and Their Makers. A Comprehensive History
Fischhof, Joseph: Versuch einer Geschichte des Clavierbaues. (Faksimile 1853).
Fuller-Maitland, J.A.: The Music of Parry and Stanford
Geminiani, Francesco: The Art of Playing the Violin.
Häuser: Musikalisches Lexikon. 2 vols in one.
Hawkins, John: A General History of the Science & Practice of Music (5 vols.)
Holmes, Edward: A Ramble among the Musicians of Germany
Hopkins, Antony: The Concertgoer's Companion - Bach to Haydn.
Hopkins, Antony: The Concertgoer's Companion – Holst to Webern.
Hopkins, Antony: Music All Around Me
Hopkins, Antony: Sounds of Music / Sounds of the Orchestra
Hopkins, Antony: The Nine Symphonies of Beethoven
Hopkins, Antony: Understanding Music

Books published by Travis & Emery Music Bookshop:

Hopkins, Edward & Rimboult, Edward: The Organ. Its History & Construction.
Hunt, John: - see separate list of discographies at the end of these titles
Iliffe, Frederick: The Forty-Eight Preludes and Fugues of John Sebastian Bach
Isaacs, Lewis: Hänsel and Gretel. A Guide to Humperdinck's Opera.
Isaacs, Lewis: Königskinder (Royal Children). Guide to Humperdinck's Opera.
Kastner: Manuel Général de Musique Militaire
Kenney, Charles Lamb: A Memoir of Michael William Balfe
Klein, Hermann: Thirty years of musical Life in London, 1870-1900
Lacassagne, M. l'Abbé Joseph : Traité Général des élémens du Chant
Lascelles (née Catley), Anne: The Life of Miss Anne Catley.
McCormack, John: John McCormack: His Own Life Story.
Mainwaring, John: Memoirs of the Life of the Late George Frederic Handel
Malcolm, Alexander: A Treaty of Music: Speculative, Practical and Historical
Manshardt, Thomas: Aspects of Cortot
Marx, Adolph Bernhard: Die Kunst des Gesanges, Theoretisch-Practisch
May, Florence: The Life of Brahms
May, Florence: The Girlhood Of Clara Schumann: Clara Wieck And Her Time.
Mellers, Wilfrid: Angels of the Night: Popular Female Singers of Our Time
Mellers, Wilfrid: Bach and the Dance of God
Mellers, Wilfrid: Beethoven and the Voice of God
Mellers, Wilfrid: Caliban Reborn - Renewal in Twentieth Century Music
Mellers, Wilfrid: Darker Shade of Pale, A Backdrop to Bob Dylan
Mellers, Wilfrid: François Couperin and the French Classical Tradition
Mellers, Wilfrid: Harmonious Meeting
Mellers, Wilfrid: Le Jardin Retrouvé, The Music of Frederic Mompou
Mellers, Wilfrid: Music and Society, England and the European Tradition
Mellers, Wilfrid: Music in a New Found Land: … … American Music
Mellers, Wilfrid: Romanticism and the Twentieth Century (from 1800)
Mellers, Wilfrid: The Masks of Orpheus: …… the Story of European Music.
Mellers, Wilfrid: The Sonata Principle (from c. 1750)
Mellers, Wilfrid: Vaughan Williams and the Vision of Albion
Newmarch, Rosa: Henry J. Wood
Newmarch, Rosa: Jean Sibelius
Newmarch, Rosa: Mary Wakefield, a Memoir
Newmarch, Rosa: The Concert-Goer's Library
Newmarch, Rosa: The Music of Czechoslovakia
Newmarch, Rosa: The Russian Opera.
Nicholas, Jeremy: Godowsky, the Pianists' Pianist
Niecks, Frederick: The Life of Chopin. (2 vols.)

Books published by Travis & Emery Music Bookshop:

Panchianio, Cattuffio: Rutzvanscad Il Giovine
Pearce, Charles: Sims Reeves, Fifty Years of Music in England.
Pepusch, John Christopher: A Treatise on Harmony ...
Pettitt, Stephen: Philharmonia Orchestra: A Record of Achievement, 1948-1985
Pettitt, Stephen (ed. Hunt): Philharmonia Orchestra: Discography 1945-1987
Playford, John: An Introduction to the Skill of Musick.
Porte, John: Sir Charles Villiers Stanford.
Quantz, Johann: Versuch einer Anweisung die Flöte traversiere zu spielen.
Rameau, Jean-Philippe: Code de Musique Pratique, ou Methodes.
Rameau, Jean-Philippe: Erreurs sur La Musique dans l'Encyclopédie
Rastall, Richard: The Notation of Western Music.
Rimbault, Edward: The Pianoforte, Its Origins, Progress, and Construction.
Rousseau, Jean Jacques: Dictionnaire de Musique
Rubinstein, Anton : Guide to the proper use of the Pianoforte Pedals.
Sainsbury, John S.: Dictionary of Musicians. (1825). (2 vols.)
Schumann, Clara & Brahms, Johannes: Letters 1853-1896. (2 vols.)
Scott-Sutherland: Arnold Bax
Serré de Rieux, Jean de : Les dons des Enfans de Latone
Simpson, Christopher: A Compendium of Practical Musick in Five Parts
Smyth, Ethel: Impressions That Remained. (2 vols.)
Spohr, Louis: Autobiography
Spohr, Louis: Grand Violin School
Tans'ur, William: A New Musical Grammar; or The Harmonical Spectator
Terry, Charles Sanford: Bach's Chorals – Parts 1, 2 and 3.
Terry, Charles Sanford: John Christian Bach
Terry, Charles Sanford: J.S. Bach's Original Hymn-Tunes - Congregational Use.
Terry, Charles Sanford: Four-Part Chorals of J.S. Bach. (German & English)
Terry, Charles Sanford: Joh. Seb. Bach, Cantata Texts, Sacred and Secular.
Terry, Charles Sanford: The Origins of the Family of Bach Musicians.
Tosi, Pierfrancesco: Opinioni de' Cantori Antichi, e Moderni
Tosi, Pierfrancesco: Observations on the Florid Song.
Tovey, Donald Francis: A Musician Talks, The Integrity of Music
Tovey, Donald Francis: A Musician Talks, Musical Textures
Tovey, Donald Francis: A Companion to "The Art of the Fugue" J.S. Bach
Tovey, Donald Francis: A Companion to Beethoven's Pianoforte Sonatas
Tovey, Donald Francis: Beethoven
Tovey, Donald Francis: Essays in Musical Analysis. (6 vols.).
Tovey, Donald Francis: The integrity of music
Tovey, Donald Francis: Musical Textures

Books published by Travis & Emery Music Bookshop:

Tovey, Donald Francis: Some English Symphonists
Tovey, Donald Francis: The Main Stream of Music.
Van der Straeten, Edmund: History of the Violoncello, The Viol da Gamba ...
Van der Straeten, Edmund: History of the Violin, Its Ancestors... (2 vols.)
Walther, J. G. [Waltern]: Musicalisches Lexikon [Musikalisches Lexicon]
Wagner, Richard: Beethoven (Leipzig 1870)
Wagner, Richard: Lebens-Bericht (Leipzig 1884)
Wagner, Richard: The Musaic of the Future (Translated by E. Dannreuther).
Wyndham, Henry Saxe: The Annals of Covent Garden Theatre. (2 vols.)
Zwirn, Gerald: Stranded Stories From The Operas

Music published by Travis & Emery Music Bookshop:

Bach, Johann Sebastian: Sacred Songs for SCTB, arranged by Franz Wullner.
Bax, Arnold: Symphony #5, Arranged for Piano Four Hands by Walter Emery
Beranger, Pierre Jean de: Musique Des Chansons de Beranger: Airs Notes ...
Bizet, Georges: Djamileh. Vocal Score.
Donizetti, Gaetano: Betly. Dramma Giocoso in Due Atti. Vocal Score.
Frescobaldi, Girolamo: D'Arie Musicali per Cantarsi. Primo & Secondo Libro.
Handel, Purcell, Boyce, Greene ... Calliope or English Harmony: Volume First.
Hopkins, Antony: Sonatine
Purcell, Henry et al: Harmonia Sacra ... The First Book, (1726)
Purcell, Henry et al: Harmonia Sacra ... Book II (1726)
Sullivan, Arthur Seymour: Ivanhoe. Vocal score.
Sullivan, Arthur Seymour: The Rose of Persia. Vocal Score.
Weckerlin, Jean-Baptiste: Chansons Populaires du Pays de France

Other Books, not on Music:

Anon: A Collection of Testimonies Concerning Several Ministers of the Gospel
          Amongst People called Quakers, Deceased. [Facsimile of 1760 edn.].
Sandeman-Allen, Arthur: Bee-keeping with Twenty hives.

Available from: Travis & Emery at 17 Cecil Court, London, UK.
(+44) (0) 20 7 240 2129. email on sales@travis-and-emery.com .

Discographies by John Hunt.

3 Italian Conductors and 7 Viennese Sopranos: 10 Discographies: Arturo Toscanini, Guido Cantelli, Carlo Maria Giulini, Elisabeth Schwarzkopf, Irmgard Seefried, Elisabeth Gruemmer, Sena Jurinac, Hilde Gueden, Lisa Della Casa, Rita Streich.

A Gallic Trio: 3 Discographies: Charles Muench, Paul Paray, Pierre Monteux.

A Notable Quartet: 4 Discographies: Gundula Janowitz, Christa Ludwig, Nicolai Gedda, Dietrich Fischer-Dieskau.

American Classics: The Discographies of Leonard Bernstein & Eugene Ormand

Antal Dorati 1906-1988: Discography and Concert Register.

Austro-Hungarian Pianists, Discographies of Lili Kraus, Friedrich Gulda, Ingrid Haebler

Back From The Shadows: 4 Discographies: Willem Mengelberg, Dimitri Mitropoulos, Hermann Abendroth, Eduard Van Beinum.

Carlo Maria Giulini: Discography and Concert Register.

Columbia 33CX Label Discography.

Concert Hall Discography: Concert Hall Society and Concert Hall Record Club

Conductors On The Yellow Label: 8 Discographies: Fritz Lehmann, Ferdinand Leitner, Ferenc Fricsay, Eugen Jochum, Leopold Ludwig, Artur Rother, Franz Konwitschny, Igor Markevitch.

Dirigenten der DDR: Conductors of the German Democratic Republic

Fremd bin ich eingezogen - a critical discography of the piano music of Franz Schubert

From Adam to Webern: the Recordings of von Karajan.

Frosh: Discography of the Richard Strauss Opera Die Frau ohne Schatten

Giants of the Keyboard: 6 Discographies: Wilhelm Kempff, Walter Gieseking, Edwin Fischer, Clara Haskil, Wilhelm Backhaus, Artur Schnabel.

Gramophone Stalwarts: 3 Separate Discographies: Bruno Walter, Erich Leinsdorf, Georg Solti.

Great Violinists: 3 Discographies: David Oistrakh, Wolfgang Schneiderhan, Arthur Grumiaux.

Hans Knappertsbusch: Kna: Concert Register and Discography of Hans Knappertsbusch, 1888-1965. Second Edition.

Her Master's Voice: Concert Register and Discography of Dame Elisabeth Schwarzkopf [Third Edition].

Hungarians in Exile: 3 Discographies: Fritz Reiner, Antal Dorati, George Szell.

Leopold Stokowski (1882-1977): Discography and Concert Register

Leopold Stokowski: Discography and Concert Listing.

Leopold Stokowski: Second Edition of the Discography.

Makers of the Philharmonia: 11 Discographies Alceo Galliera, Walter Susskind, Paul Kletzki, Nicolai Malko, Issay Dobrowen, Lovro Von Matacic, Efrem Kurtz, Otto Ackermann, Anatole Fistoulari, George Weldon, Robert Irving.

Metropolitan Sopranos: 4 Discographies: Rosa Ponselle, Eleanor Steber, Zinka Milanov, Leontyne Price.

Mezzo and Contraltos: 5 Discographies: Janet Baker, Margarete Klose, Kathleen Ferrier, Giulietta Simionato, Elisabeth Hoengen.

Mid-Century Conductors and More Viennese Singers: 10 Discographies: Karl Boehm, Victor De Sabata, Hans Knappertsbusch, Tullio Serafin, Clemens Krauss, Anton Dermota, Leonie Rysanek, Eberhard Waechter, Maria Reining, Erich Kunz.

More 20th Century Conductors: 7 Discographies: Eugen Jochum, Ferenc Fricsay, Carl Schuricht, Felix Weingartner, Josef Krips, Otto Klemperer, Erich Kleiber.

More Giants of the Keyboard: 5 Discographies: Claudio Arrau, Gyorgy Cziffra, Vladimir Horowitz, Dinu Lipatti, Artur Rubinstein.

More Musical Knights: 4 Discographies: Hamilton Harty, Charles Mackerras, Simon Rattle, John Pritchard.

Musical Knights: 6 Discographies: Henry Wood, Thomas Beecham, Adrian Boult, John Barbirolli, Reginald Goodall, Malcolm Sargent.

Philharmonic Autocrat 1: Discography of: Herbert Von Karajan [3rd Edition]

Philharmonic Autocrat 2: Concert Register of Herbert Von Karajan 2nd. Ed.

Philharmonic Autocrat: Discography of Herbert von Karajan (1908-1989). 4th Ed..

Philharmonisches Orchester Berlin, the historic years, 1913-1954

Philips Minigroove: Second Extended Version of the European Discography.

Pianists For The Connoisseur: 6 Discographies: Arturo Benedetti Michelangeli, Alfred Cortot, Alexis Weissenberg, Clifford Curzon, Solomon, Elly Ney.

Record Pioneers: Richard Strauss, Hans Pfitzner, Oskar Fried, Oswald Kabasta, Karl Muck, Franz Von Hoesslin, Karl Elmendorff.

Sächsische Staatskapelle Dresden: Complete Discography.

Singers of the Third Reich: 5 Discographies: Helge Roswaenge, Tiana Lemnitz, Franz Voelker, Maria Mueller, Max Lorenz.

Singers on the Yellow Label: 7 Discographies: Maria Stader, Elfriede Troetschel, Annelies Kupper, Wolfgang Windgassen, Ernst Haefliger, Josef Greindl, Kim Borg

Six Wagnerian Sopranos: 6 Discographies: Frieda Leider, Kirsten Flagstad, Astrid Varnay, Martha Moedl, Birgit Nilsson, Gwyneth Jones.

Staatskapelle Berlin. The shellac era 1916-1962.

Sviatoslav Richter: Pianist of the Century: Discography.

Teachers and Pupils: 7 Discographies: Elisabeth Schwarzkopf, Maria Ivoguen, Maria Cebotari, Meta Seinemeyer, Ljuba Welitsch, Rita Streich, Erna Berger

Tenors in a Lyric Tradition: 3 Discographies: Peter Anders, Walther Ludwig, Fritz Wunderlich.

The Art of the Diva: 3 Discographies: Claudia Muzio, Maria Callas, Magda Olivero.

The Furtwaengler Sound Sixth Edition: Discography and Concert Listing.

The Furtwängler Sound. Discography of Wilhelm Furtwängler. Seventh Edition.

The Great Dictators: 3 Discographies: Evgeny Mravinsky, Artur Rodzinski, Sergiu Celibidache.

The Lyric Baritone: 5 Discographies: Hans Reinmar, Gerhard Huesch, Josef Metternich, Hermann Uhde, Eberhard Waechter.

The Post-War German Tradition: 5 Discographies: Rudolf Kempe, Joseph Keilberth, Wolfgang Sawallisch, Rafael Kubelik, Andre Cluytens.

Wagner Im Festspielhaus: Discography of the Bayreuth Festival.

Wiener Philharmoniker 1 - Vienna Philharmonic and Vienna State Opera Orchestras: Discography Part 1 1905-1954.

Wiener Philharmoniker 2 - Vienna Philharmonic and Vienna State Opera Orchestras: Discography Part 2 1954-1989.

Wiener Staatsoper: 348 complete relays

Available from: Travis & Emery at 17 Cecil Court, London, UK. (+44) (0) 20 7 240 2129. email on sales@travis-and-emery.com .

© Travis & Emery 2018

www.ingramcontent.com/pod-product-compliance
Lightning Source LLC
Chambersburg PA
CBHW052040230426
43671CB00011B/1723